EMILY CARTER

DBT
WORKBOOK
for Teens

Easy & Proven Ways to Manage Anger, Anxiety & Stress, Improve Communication Skills, and Develop Healthy Coping Skills for Better Emotional Regulation Using Mindfulness & DBT

TABLE OF CONTENTS

YOUR FREE GIFT

To really make the most out of your life, and to succeed in it, it's crucial to never stop learning. To further develop your knowledge of important life skills, I've got something for you... something you can really be excited about!

As a way of saying thank you for your purchase, I want to offer you some BONUSES completely FREE of charge:

To get instant access, just go to:

https://lifeskillbooks.com

Here's just a glimpse of what is included:

BONUS 1

Unleashing Your Potential: A Teenager's Guide to Developing a Growth Mindset and Opening Your Path to Success

Inside the book, you will discover...

✦ The differences between a fixed and growth mindset, how your mindset impacts your personal growth and success, and why a growth mindset is the one you should adopt.

✦ Practical strategies to cultivate a growth mindset, from daily habits to overcoming obstacles.

✦ How to utilize a growth mindset to supercharge your academic and career success.

✦ And much more!

BONUS 2

The Anxiety Handbook: Understand the Types, Triggers and Symptoms of Anxiety to Effectively Cope With It

Inside this comprehensive guide, you will discover...

✦ Insights into different types of anxiety disorders, so you can understand and identify specific triggers.

✦ Overview of the symptoms of each anxiety type so you can learn to recognize them better.

✦ Proven techniques to manage and reduce anxiety, helping you regain control over your life.

✦ And more!

BONUS 3

Printable Self-Regulation & Coping Skills Worksheets: Practical Tools for Managing Stress, Anxiety and Emotions

Inside this comprehensive workbook, you will discover...

◇ **Step-by-Step Coping Strategies**: Gain access to structured exercises that help you identify, challenge, and reframe negative thoughts, leading to a more positive mindset.

◇ **Personalized Mood and Habit Tracking**: Utilize detailed trackers to monitor your mood and daily habits, allowing you to identify patterns and make informed changes for better mental health.

◇ **Self-Care and Mindfulness Practices**: Engage in a 30-day self-care challenge and explore various self-soothing techniques to promote relaxation and reduce stress.

- ✧ **Interactive and Easy-to-Use Worksheets**: Enjoy a user-friendly layout with guided prompts and questions designed to support your journey toward improved mental well-being and personal growth.

- ✧ **And more!** Everything is in easily printable form.

Now, go to the website below for instant access to these and several other amazing bonuses. Completely free of charge.

https://lifeskillbooks.com

INTRODUCTION

"Life is a balance of holding on and letting go."

– Rumi

You are about to begin a journey of self-discovery. I know you. You've come from a challenging place and want to see how to deal with whatever life throws at you differently. Being a teenager is one of the most challenging things you have gone through in life so far. As you navigate this exciting phase, you notice changes happening all around you – the dynamic in your family changes, your friendships grow and change, you enter a new school environment, and you also change and grow as a person, as well. You've probably even felt lost and insecure at times. That's why I'm here to give you a hand.

Don't think of this book as another self-help book. Think of it as a friend – one who will guide you through this exciting chapter of your life designed specifically for you. Here, you will learn what it takes to be a teenager in this world and how to find yourself, center yourself, and to simply – be yourself. The skills I focused on in this book are based on Dialectical Behavior Therapy (DBT). This powerful approach can help you manage your emotions and build your entire life from the ground up.

Understanding Dialectical Behavior Therapy

Dialectical Behavior Therapy, or DBT, is a type of cognitive-behavioral therapy that was originally developed to help people manage their intense emotions. Nowadays, it is the perfect tool for young people like you to develop some strong skills. DBT is built on the idea that two things can coexist and be true at the same time. A good example of this would be, accepting yourself for who you are but also wanting to change yourself. The balance between these two is what DBT is all about.

Right now, you feel like there is a rollercoaster of emotions – one minute, you feel like you are on top of the world, and the next minute, you feel like all is falling apart. The good news is that DBT will help you navigate these highs and lows even when you're struggling with stress, sadness, anxiety, or just the regular changes that happen within you while growing up. The DBT skills can help you collect all the tools you need at your disposal to tackle anything that comes your way.

Before we begin, it is crucial for you to understand that DBT consists of four concepts. These concepts are - mindfulness, distress tolerance, emotional intelligence, and interpersonal effectiveness. We are going to go through all of these concepts together. Just to give you an idea of what each of these represent, here are some brief explanations.

Mindfulness is the art of being fully focused and present in the moment. It consists of observing, describing, and participating without any judgement. It is considered the foundation of DBT. Through it, you can enhance your awareness and allow yourself to recognize your own thoughts.

Distress tolerance is knowing how to survive and cope with difficult situations. Here, it is all about soothing yourself and accepting the situation as it is. Life can deal you with some tough cards sometimes, and distress tolerance is important so that you can learn how to survive during these moments without engaging in harmful behaviors.

Emotional regulation is the ability to manage your emotions in what is considered a healthy way. Identifying and managing your emotional responses is crucial if you want to maintain emotional balance. This way, you can enhance your overall well-being.

Finally, interpersonal effectiveness is knowing how to communicate with other people in a way that exudes confidence and respect. As an aspect of DBT, it can help you navigate social situations and build long-lasting relationships.

All of these concepts tie together to create a comprehensive framework that will help you deal with any kind of emotional challenge that comes your way. As you go through this book, you will notice how strong and important they are.

How to Use This Workbook?

Using this workbook to your advantage will be easier said than done in some situations. But, looking at the bigger picture, you will realize that this book is meticulously divided into sections that focus on the core DBT skills. Every section comes with incredible explanations, is easy enough to understand and implement, and is filled with exercises and examples. These can help you apply what you've learned in real-life situations. To answer your question of how to use this workbook, the best way to do that is through the exercises. They are extremely beneficial, and all you need to do in most of them is to take notes, and sometimes have a partner to talk to (depending on the exercise).

Through the book, you will find many ways to use DBT skills to overcome the challenges you're faced with in life every day. Some of the examples can be your reassurance – you're not alone, and you've never been alone in this.

Before we dive right into the subject, let me tell you something important – you already are as capable and strong as you wish. Just think about this – you are here, reading this introduction, getting ready to read the book that will ultimately shape your life. You are ready to take control. The path is filled with obstacles. It will not be easy. Sometimes, you may want to give up, but I am here to help you power through and make it to the other side. This book is designed to help you every step of the way.

Work through these skills, make mistakes along the way, and allow yourself to grow. Be patient, as change takes a lot of time. Count all small steps you take as victories and get ready to start the journey – because now, it is time for you to turn the page and begin!

Part 1

MINDFULNESS

"To a mind that is still, the whole universe surrenders."

– Lao Tzu

There is a certain connection between your mind and your relationship with yourself and everything else around you. This certain kind of connection you have is special. It is unique, and depending on how well you nurture it, it will either flourish or perish.

In this first part, we will talk about mindfulness and how to stop whatever you are doing and start focusing on yourself. Because remember, the star of this book is you. The work you will be doing while reading is unmatched – and you will only get to realize that once you are done with the last page. I will have managed to describe every aspect you should focus on. Now, it is yours to accept and grasp the term mindfulness with both hands.

But that's not all. In this part, I will help you explore a few other important aspects of DBT - these include the wise mind, the what skills, and the how skills. You might see them as confusing terms now. However, as we delve deeper into the book together, you will notice how all of them are connected. There is not one without the other. It is all about getting a better understanding of what lies ahead for you. While you want to paint the big picture now, remember that any big picture consists of small things. From mindfulness, to the how skills, these are the small, yet significant things you are going to explore.

What Is Mindfulness?

Mindfulness. This word signifies an incredible concept of being fully present in the moment. It elaborates on the fact that your mind is completely present. Whether you are doing something, moving through a certain space, or you are fully invested in what is going on.

For a young mind such as yours, this may seem like a strange concept. You may even ask, "Well, isn't my mind present all the time?" and you are right to do so. It may even sound illogical as a statement, except it isn't. The mind works all the time, and often, it can steer us away from the moment we're currently in. You've probably felt it before – it simply takes off in the middle of a situation, and you start to lose touch with your senses, your body, and so on. As soon as you know it, this is something that can make you feel absent in an instant.

Sit with this for a while, has this ever happened to you? It must have at some point by now. That is why I am starting this book with the concept of mindfulness. Because everything you will ever learn from this point on connects back to it. Mindfulness is more than the human ability to be fully present in the moment – it is the pillar upon which this book is based.

The good thing about mindfulness is that you already have it within you. This is not something you need to work to obtain (like a degree), it is already present. All you need to do is learn how to access it and nurture it.

Are you still feeling a little bit confused? I've created a small list of things that can help you understand the concept of mindfulness. Think of them as facts, something that cannot be changed.

- ✦ Mindfulness is a familiar thing. You already do this every day, but up until now, you haven't been aware of it.

- ✦ Mindfulness is not some special thing you can be or do. You hold a spectacular power to be present within yourself, and you do not need to change to harness it. All you need to do is cultivate it.

- ✦ Mindfulness recognizes your full potential. Every solution that requires change from you should not be implemented. Mindfulness helps you cultivate the best of who you are as a human being.

- ✦ Anyone can do mindfulness – specifically because it has the potential to grow into a transformative phenomenon. You can really benefit from it, and it is an easy thing to focus on.

- ✧ You can easily turn mindfulness into a lifestyle. It is more than just a practice. By doing that, you will slowly implement a caring and an awareness approach to every aspect of your life.
- ✧ It will spark up your entire life. Mindfulness comes with many benefits, including happiness, improved relationships, better work, wilder imagination, and innovation, as well as effectiveness and resilience.

But of course, you are not here to learn just about mindfulness. We both know that this is only the beginning. Next, you are going to delve a little bit deeper into your mind.

WISE MIND

Wise mind - more famously known as the "aha" moment in DBT. I already mentioned that DBT is an abbreviation for dialectical behavior therapy. It is kind of like a talk therapy that can help you understand your emotions as well as your behavior. Within this book, you are going to learn how to incorporate that into your everyday life. Remember that the whole purpose of DBT is to help you accept the reality of your life and your behavior as well as to help you enjoy it to the fullest extent.

I am aware that until this point, everything sounds completely new to you, but you will soon find out that everything serves its own purpose. And the wise mind is only the first concept for you to understand. Well, a wise mind is not something you have. It is a technique. The wise mind is the core aspect of DBT, and it is based on the concept that there are three states of mind – a reasonable mind, an emotional mind, and a wise mind.

The wise mind represents the absolute optimal state. This is the place where emotions and rational thinking come together. The wise mind allows an individual to make a solid and sound decision based on both, so it is something that aligns with their goals and values. As a technique, the wise mind is very successful and powerful because it can help you strengthen your mind, especially when you are feeling a little distressed. It includes mindfulness exercises so you can make the most out of any situation.

The good thing about the wise mind is that it comes with many qualities and characteristics. By cultivating it, you can navigate many challenges that come your way. Here are some of them:

- ✧ You get to work on your intuition. The wise mind technique can help you get a better understanding of what comes within you and can guide you toward taking the appropriate action.

✧ After using it for a while, your ability to clearly see any situation or issue is improved. You are objective and don't allow strong emotions to overwhelm you.

✧ The wise mind is the perfect way to incorporate some balance into your life. The reason behind this is to incorporate both the rational and the emotional aspects, helping you find the exact middle between them.

✧ As you incorporate the wise mind technique into your life, you open yourself up to an authentic experience. Instead of being led by external factors, you delve deep into your true, authentic self.

✧ A life of compassion is what follows. Cultivating the wise mind means you will foster a feeling of empathy, understanding, and compassion – both toward yourself and others.

It seems that navigating challenges will be easy after reading this, right? We are only at the beginning, so let's move on to discovering how to integrate both the reasonable and the emotional mind.

As a concept, the wise mind relies on the merging of the reasonable and the emotional mind. The reasonable mind is the analytical one, the one that looks at every situation logically, while the emotional mind represents the intuitive aspect of it all. When you combine the two together, you can make sound decisions.

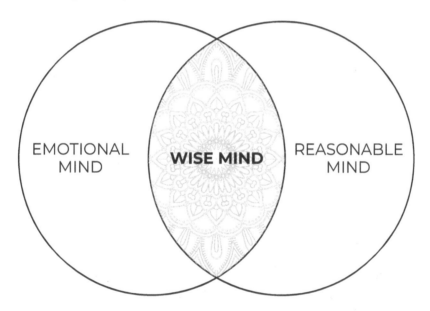

There is an importance behind doing this. By balancing the reasonable and the emotional mind, you can start effectively solving problems and making decisions. Why is that so? Well, think about it. Say you need to make a decision. A large one. If you only look at it from a logical point of view, you may come to a very robotic and detached solution. But on the other hand, if you only include your emotional side in it, you might make an impulsive and irrational decision.

That's why I love to focus on both aspects. While doing that, you discover a whole new part of yourself too – a balanced one. Using the wise mind means you consider your goals and values, but also your well-being. And once you find it – you never go back.

You learn that when emotions are the only thing driving your decisions, you may become moody and reactive and act in a way that is not really typical for you. As you are a teenager, I can understand how emotions can get in the way sometimes. That's probably the main reason why you started reading this book in the first place. Without the help of a little bit of logic, you will only rely on your impulsivity.

It is time to take a look at the first exercise.

EXERCISE 1
IDENTIFYING AND ACCESSING THE WISE MIND

The first of the many exercises you will find throughout this book is identifying and accessing the wise mind. As you can see, we already explored the topics of reasonable and emotional mind – now it is time to put them both to good use!

As you can see, cultivating mindfulness is a crucial thing if you want to access the wise mind. You need to be present in the moment and be attentive – fully aware of your feelings, thoughts, and body. I mentioned earlier that it is all about balance – the perfect combination between emotion and reason. Here is how you can identify and access your wise mind.

It is all about using mindfulness. Find a space where you feel comfortable and do the following (you can either sit down or do this standing up):

- ✧ Take a minute to pause and take a deep breath.
- ✧ Clear your mind from everything, and focus on you, both physically and mentally, in that moment.
- ✧ Focus on the current thing that constantly occupies your mind. This can be anything - an idea, a plan, or maybe an emotion.
- ✧ Sit with it for a minute and recognize it fully. Allow yourself to recognize the sensations you have with that idea or thought in your mind.
- ✧ Now, it is time to access the wise mind.
- ✧ Ask yourself, "How can I benefit from this plan/idea/action/thought? Is this connected to my wise mind?"

- ✧ Allow yourself to listen to both the emotion and the logic. The answer is somewhere in between. If it helps, take notes.
- ✧ Before you finish this thought process, check if the decision you are making causes you any imbalance of emotion or reason. Remember, the wise mind should also give you peace of mind.

If you don't know how to check in with yourself, it is always good to follow the breadcrumbs – your body. I have noticed that many people, especially young people, experience the wise mind in the center of their body or between the eyes. To complete the process, try to allow yourself to enter a meditative state. Try to intentionally bring awareness to these body parts and see how you feel. Notice the thoughts and the feelings. If you are making the right decision, you will feel calmer, centered and ready to get back into reality.

_____

_____

_____

_____

_____

_____

_____

_____

_____

_____

_____

_____

_____

_____

_____

_____

_____

_____

_____

_____

_____

_____

_____

_____

As you continue reading, you will discover a lot of new things about yourself. And I will be there every step of the way, making it easier for you to understand the process of balancing yourself and your emotions. The next thing we're going to look into is the mindfulness skills. These are considered the foundation of all DBT skills. They are also known under a different name – the what skills and the how skills. Remember earlier in the chapter, when I mentioned this? Well, first off, we are going to start with the what skills, and then we are going to move on to the how skills.

WHAT SKILLS

The issues that are addressed with these mindfulness skills can help you know who you are, what you want to do with your life, and how to obtain it. These skills can even help you control what's going on in your mind. The "what" part from the what skills refers to the ways of practicing your thinking – what you do to take control over yourself. The three ways that I'm about to share with you are important, and all of them can help you whenever you are dealing with an issue or need a change. They are - observing, describing, and participating. I will go into detail for each of them below.

01.

Observing

Observing is about being present in the moment and opening up all of your senses to every experience - your touch, sight, smell, taste, and hearing. The lens of your senses can be extremely powerful, and during the observation of the present moment, you utilize all of them. When you observe, you experience without ever labelling the experience. In the beginning, you may find yourself struggling with this, and that's okay. After a while, you will notice the quiet benefits of this skill. You will learn how to observe without your mind talking as much.

It will be difficult for you to watch thoughts go by, as there is always a little bit of temptation included, which is also something that can help you get "caught up" in the experience. When you get caught up, this may mean you are becoming obsessed, where you preoccupy yourself with something, and you can't stop thinking about it. With the power of observation, the goal is to stand back a little bit. I do not want you to detach from the situation entirely but rather take a step back and try to view it objectively.

Another thing here – I know it is tempting for you to react to every thought you have in this situation – especially to the negative ones. These thoughts can make you want to leave a specific situation. But the challenge of being observant means experiencing something without judging whether it is good or bad. In this situation, you let all the thoughts go by.

EXERCISE 2
BODY SCAN

Let's make two exercises connected to this observing skill. In this first exercise, I advise you to sit down, or even lay down on a yoga mat or a carpet. Try to completely relax and feel yourself, your entire body. Focus on your breath and notice how your body inflates and deflates with every breathing cycle. Now, you should do a body scan. Start from the top (or from the bottom) and work your way through every part of your body. Really feel and pay attention to every part of your body - arms, legs, torso, hair, neck, everything.

Now, notice your thought pattern. You are a teenager, so chances are – there is something about yourself that you don't like. Say, for example, you don't like your legs. As soon as you think about them, you immediately have negative feelings. By using the power of observation, notice these thoughts – but allow them to flow through you rather than being stuck with them. It may take you a while to get there, so I recommend you practice this whenever you get a chance.

When I want to connect with myself, I always start from the bottom and work my way up. If you don't know where to begin, this is a good starting point. Start from the feet and feel them (one at a time). Consider this to be almost of a spiritual practice. While you observe, you also connect on the highest possible level. The goal here is to be connected with every part of your body, know all its edges and how they make you feel. Now, we were talking about the feet. Start with whichever one you like, and really feel it. Is it in pain, is it pulsating (maybe if you've walked for a longer time before you did this exercise)? Acknowledge any sensations you feel around it - is it cold, hot, or incredibly comfortable? Do you have a sock on your foot? How does that feel too? This exercise is all about becoming more aware of sensory experiences - and ultimately, more accepting of them. This exercise is about training the mind rather than relaxing it. After a short while, you will see how it makes you feel a little more centered, and helps you connect to any sensations you're feeling without judging them.

EXERCISE 3
OBSERVING THE SURROUNDINGS

It is interesting to see how many things surround us. These things are incredible – just take a look at what surrounds you at the moment. It seems almost incredible, right? In this exercise, it is about observing your environment. For example, if you are at home, during the day, or in the office, find a sunny spot. Give it a minute and notice the sun's rays penetrating through the windows and illuminating the room. Allow the opinions to wash over you once again, and to let them flow.

On the other hand, if you are outside, try to be even more observant. Do the surroundings change often (meaning – are you a part of a crowd)? Or maybe you're in a park? Observe with all of your senses, and allow the feelings to sink in.

02.

Describing

The next skill we're talking about is describing. This, in simple terms, means putting into words what you have observed. However, it still means describing an experience without any judgment.

This act of describing the responses and the things that happen around you (or to you) can provide you with the ability to label events and behaviors. When you start describing a situation that makes you feel a certain way (either good or bad), it helps you observe it more objectively and make a clear connection between yourself and what surrounds you or what is happening.

The goal here is to use the skills of observation and description together to help you stay in the present moment. Together, they will provide you with the focus you need.

EXERCISE 4
DESCRIBING THOUGHTS, FEELINGS, AND SENSATIONS

It is important to learn how to describe everything you think and feel – and not consider those things as facts. Your state will constantly change, and for example, if you feel afraid, it does not necessarily mean that there is a real danger around you. So, in this exercise, you will learn how to describe your thoughts, feelings, and sensations.

Pick one thing that you do every day – your morning or night routine, cooking a meal, walking, or playing with your pet – yes, this can be anything. Start by observing the experience while you are doing it. As you notice every single detail (even some details you have missed before), start describing the experience without judging it. For example, you might be one of those people who don't close the toothpaste after using it – and you might associate that with a feeling of laziness or indifference. Try to remove these "obstacles" and just describe to yourself what you are doing. Describe the experience, the sensations, every little thing.

_____

_____

_____

_____

_____

_____

_____

_____

_____

_____

_____

_____

_____

_____

_____

_____

_____

_____

_____

_____

It is quite a revelation when you look at what you have described. This will give you a sense of who you are, what interests you, and what you notice the most, as well as give you an insight into your thought pattern. Except in this situation, it will look as if you have taken a step back and you are looking at the situation objectively – meaning you're on the right path.

EXERCISE 5
"I FEEL" STATEMENTS

Now, take things a step further – and feel.

During this exercise, we are going to label emotions. There are probably at least a handful of times in life when you felt disappointed, happy, sad, angry, content, etc. In this fifth exercise, you will learn how to verbally describe your feelings in a given moment.

This is an exercise you can do next time you find yourself in a situation that makes you feel a certain way. Until now, you have most likely relied on the factor of the emotional mind, leading to a possible outburst in many situations. But now, try to do this exercise. Something happens to you – maybe a friend or a sibling tells you something you don't like, or a situation starts making you feel uncomfortable. Rather than an outburst and creating an even bigger situation, try to step back and – use the wise mind. Observe whatever you think and feel during that given moment, and then state it. Make the "I feel" statement. Say, "I feel sad you acted that way", or "I feel disappointed in you."

Let's try to put this into perspective by examples. The "I feel," statements would be ones that reflect your present state, but they should be ones you realize will pass and will be resolved with time. So, here are a few examples of when a bad scenario presents itself before you. This is the best time to use these statements. You can also use the following for practice.

1. When you get caught up in a verbal altercation with a friend.
2. When you notice that your parents are pushing you to your limit.
3. When you have a misunderstanding with your sibling.
4. When you expected someone to do something for you, and they failed to deliver.
5. When someone promised you something, but they didn't fulfill it.

6. When you feel cornered by a teacher or educator because of a certain thing you did or didn't do.

7. When you are all alone with yourself, and you have this surge of negative feelings coming on.

8. When your romantic interest is not interested in you anymore.

9. When you feel trapped in a social situation.

10. When your best friend does something to you, intentionally (or not).

These sayings come from a valid point – but saying them out loud not only helps you create a better communication channel with someone else but also with yourself. These sayings are also a reflection of what is happening at the moment. They are not facts; they are just thoughts or feelings, so there is no need to cling to them like facts. I would encourage you to put them on paper as this is the easiest way to exercise them. Write down the "I feel" statements and keep doing that until you feel comfortable with yourself to communicate them with the people around you.

Situation: _____

I feel... _____

_____

_____

Situation: _____

I feel... _____

_____

_____

Situation: _____

I feel... _____

_____

_____

_____

Situation: _____

I feel... _____

_____

_____

_____

Situation: _____

I feel... _____

_____

_____

_____

Situation: _____

I feel... _____

_____

_____

_____

Situation: _____

I feel... _____

_____

_____

_____

Situation: _____

I feel... _____

_____

_____

_____

Situation: _____

I feel... _____

_____

_____

_____

Situation: _____

I feel... _____

_____

_____

_____

Situation: _____

I feel... _____

_____

_____

_____

Situation: _____

I feel... _____

_____

_____

_____

Situation: _____

I feel... _____

_____

_____

_____

Situation: _____

I feel... _____

_____

_____

_____

Situation: _____

I feel... _____

_____

_____

_____

Situation: _____

I feel... _____

_____

_____

_____

Situation: _____

I feel... _____

_____

_____

_____

03.

Participating

The final "what" skill we're going to dissect is the participating skill. It means completely immersing yourself in a certain activity. It means jumping head-first and allowing yourself to be involved in the moment. Doing this helps you to let go of self-consciousness and be completely present in whichever activity you're indulging in. When you participate with awareness, you can completely enjoy the moment without having to overthink every step of the way or be "half-present" in the moment. Participating is an excellent skill to use if you are feeling stressed.

In order to participate, all you need to do is actively practice the other skills and then immerse yourself in this one. Instead of closing this cycle with dissociation and not really remembering or enjoying something, do the opposite. Participate. This is the perfect way to start actively practicing these DBT skills until they become a part of who you are.

EXERCISE 6
MINDFUL PRACTICE

That leads us to the sixth exercise. Mindful practice means being active and aware. For this exercise, try to do something that you do often (like washing the dishes, eating, or something else). But this time, try to pay full attention to everything. Concentrate as hard as you can and notice every single thing you're doing. Then, try to do every single thing as well as you can. Take washing a piece of fruit as an example. Take the fruit (let's say it's a pear), go to your kitchen sink, and turn on the faucet. This is something you unconsciously do every time - but in this case, try to feel the whole process. Do you turn the water all the way to the coldest or the hottest point? Or do you maybe rinse your piece of fruit with lukewarm water? How does it feel? Notice the water going through your hands and between your fingers, onto the skin of the pear. Notice how gentle you are so you don't damage the fruit. Be as specific as you can while doing this task. Then, take a pen and write down how this made you feel - being mindful and completely present in the moment.

Activity: _____

How being mindful made me feel: _____

_____

_____

_____

Activity: _____

How being mindful made me feel: _____

_____

_____

_____

Activity: _____

How being mindful made me feel: _____

_____

_____

_____

Activity: _____

How being mindful made me feel: _____

_____

_____

_____

Activity: _____

How being mindful made me feel: _____

_____

_____

_____

Activity: _____

How being mindful made me feel: _____

_____

_____

_____

Activity: _____

How being mindful made me feel: _____

_____

_____

_____

Activity: _____

How being mindful made me feel: _____

_____

_____

_____

As I mentioned earlier, the basis of everything in this book revolves around the concept of mindfulness. The skills we're looking into together are all connected to it, and they are considered the foundation of DBT. After reading through the what skills, you are probably aware of what I'm talking about. You've probably noticed that the issues addressed by these skills will help you realize who you are and what you want out of life. These skills will also help you control what's happening in your mind, resulting in you living in the moment and focusing on the now.

HOW SKILLS

The second set of skills we will tackle are the how skills. These are just as important as the what skills, and their focus is helping you practice mindfulness. DBT has truly paved the way for any person to develop themselves into the form they want, and these skills are the perfect beginning to that adventure! To deepen your practice, you should follow these three skills that I have outlined for you below. They are – nonjudgmentally, one-mindfully, and effectively.

01.

Nonjudgmentally

The first one is being nonjudgmental. As people, all we do is judge – especially teenagers. But if you are a person who is constantly judged for your behavior, looks, or anything else – you will probably understand this the most. After all, you are in the middle of those teenage years where, frankly – kids can be mean.

I am sorry to be the bearer of bad news, but judgment continues throughout your entire life. You judge others, but mostly, you judge yourself. The thing is, you need to understand that judgment as a form can possibly lead to the creation of a highly hostile environment – both inside and outside your body. It can lead to guilt, shame, sadness, and so much more.

That's why I would like to dedicate some time to learning how not to judge. The point here is to allow yourself to observe everything you've observed until now but open up to a different kind of thinking. It is not about withholding your judgment but rather understanding it. Observe your thoughts as if you are observing a different person. Treat yourself more gently. The judgemental thoughts will slowly start to fade away because, at given moments, you will begin practicing the most powerful act – of letting go.

EXERCISE 7
PRACTICING SELF-COMPASSION

I mentioned that the most judgment you are ever going to receive in your life is judgment from yourself. As human beings, we are all flawed, but it seems like we keep forgetting that at times. That is why I designed this exercise – to remind you that, if you want to make sure you're viewing the world with compassion, you need to begin with yourself.

Say you're trying to observe a situation, and it is just not working out for you. You keep getting distracted, and other things keep popping up in your mind. You start to spiral, and before you know it, you blame yourself for your entire behavior without ever giving yourself the benefit of the doubt.

The exercise is as follows – you notice that you are starting to go down that rabbit hole, but you don't know how to stop. Start by noticing every sentence that goes through your mind and every negative thought about yourself. With each sentence, take a step back and analyze it. Here's a small example of it. You start thinking about that friend who let you down or said something mean to you. Then, you start thinking about whether they actually don't like you (or maybe they never did?). This is the time when you need to stop going down the rabbit hole, because you are practically spiralling - you start thinking you don't have any friends, or that this particular friend doesn't care about you, and so on. Bring yourself back to the surface by reminding yourself that anyone can have thoughts and feelings that do not coincide with yours at some point.

Then, ask yourself this – are each of those spiralling thoughts true? Or is it something that is derived from the emotional mind (which is usually activated when we don't have full control over a situation)? Remember to do this every time you feel like your self-compassion levels are low. Below, you can find some lines to take notes.

_____

_____

_____

_____

_____

_____

_____

_____

_____

_____

_____

_____

_____

_____

_____

_____

_____

_____

EXERCISE 8
CHALLENGE JUDGMENTS

Challenging yourself about yourself is one thing – but challenging yourself about judgments towards the outside world is a whole new thing. In this exercise, let's try to do that together, shall we?

Say you're in a situation where you're meeting a new person – and you instantly start to judge them. Once you notice yourself doing this, it means you are on the right path of mindfulness. Notice all the thoughts going through your mind and witness how they form. Question them. Why are you thinking this? Is the person standing opposite you really that bad? Or is it something that may have derived from another experience you've had with another person in the past – that reminded you of them? It is important to start recognizing these thoughts in your head. Don't forget to take notes of your observations.

_____

_____

_____

_____

_____

_____

02.

One-Mindfully

The second one is one-mindfully. This is a skill that will come up as you are reading this book in one way or another. The idea behind it is that whatever you are doing, you should be doing one thing at a time. It is about finding mindfulness in everything you do. For example, if you are learning, reading, or working, do that. Don't play music in the background. Try not to turn the TV on or have some kind of other noise happening. Or when you're with someone else, say a friend, try to be with them, present in the moment, instead of constantly looking at your phone.

The idea behind this is that you can give your full attention to something and do your best to maintain it. Doing this will help you stay in the present moment rather than having your attention divided all over the place. So, you see, mindfulness truly has a lot to do with the level of awareness you bring into your life. Focusing on being present in the moment, giving your undivided attention to what you are doing – there is no greater feeling than that. Most of us, all through our lives, are distracted. Whether it is by images, feelings, thoughts, or even worries – we constantly try ways to steer clear of the present moment. Once you get used to this, it's a little challenging to put everything away and focus on only one thing.

Being one-mindfully is an excellent way to pull your attention to what is happening at the moment. With it, you can absorb the information and take part in the present.

However, the most important thing to remember here is that you always need to be patient with yourself. It takes time to master this skill, and while some of you may achieve this in a shorter time period, others may need some more time. In the beginning, if you're having trouble focusing on a task, try to remove all the distractions from your surroundings. Observe everything that surrounds you and pinpoint the things you need to remove. Choose one thing that you'd like to focus on and start doing it slowly. With time, this will become an unconscious process.

EXERCISE 9
FOCUS YOUR ATTENTION ON ONE THING
AT A TIME

That is precisely why I have chosen this to be an exercise as well. In life, sometimes you need to stand still and let go of every thought and emotion. It is with this exercise that you're going to do just that. Let's try focusing your attention on one thing at a time.

Stand in the middle of a room. You don't even have to do anything – just watch. Now, choose a couple of objects around the room. Then, try to focus on one subject (say, a chair). Take a deep look at the chair and try not to think of anything else. Notice the materials, the patterns, the shapes – pay full attention to the chair. At that moment, you should completely forget about the other items you've chosen or that there is anything else in the room. After you've observed one thing, try to shift your focus to another thing. Do this process with a few objects just to get started. Before you know it, you will be able to do this in a heartbeat, with everything.

03.

Effectively

The third one is effectively. As a word, effective is something you're going to hear a lot. The goal here is to know you're effective every time you focus on what works. Instead of thinking whether something is right or wrong, you should focus on understanding how to accept and work with a situation as it is. Effectively means allowing yourself to let go of the need to be right. When you are determined to be right, it may cloud your judgment and make you come to the wrong conclusion or decision. Being determined to be right all the time can be a very challenging thing.

Effectiveness is knowing how to tolerate and accept a situation or a person you don't really like. Effectiveness is knowing you are right but still letting go because fighting something and proving how right you are don't really align with your values anymore. You are simply – better than that. By accepting a situation where you know you can't change things, you show the actual signs of growth.

EXERCISE 10
ALIGNING ACTIONS WITH
VALUES AND GOALS

For the last exercise of this chapter, you are going to need a pen. The goal is to access your values, and then make goals based on them. But, to assess your values, you need to start somewhere, right? Well, start by thinking about the values that you hold in your life. Now start writing. Let's go step by step.

Think about what matters most to you in life. Write down 5-10 values that come to mind. These can be anything. Here are some examples:

✧ I value respect for myself and others.

✧ Gratitude for what I have is important to me.

✧ I believe in the strength to overcome challenges.

✧ I value honesty and being true to myself.

✧ I care deeply about kindness and helping others.

MY VALUES

1. _____

2. _____

3. _____

4. _____

5. _____

6. _____

7. _____

8. _____

9. _____

10. _____

Based on the values you wrote down, create goals that reflect them. Here are a few examples:

- ✧ If you value respect, a goal could be to strengthen your relationships.
- ✧ If you value success, you might set a goal to achieve something specific in your studies.
- ✧ If you value gratitude, your goal could be to practice it daily.
- ✧ If you value honesty, a goal could be to communicate more openly with people.
- ✧ If kindness matters to you, a goal might be to volunteer or support a cause regularly.

MY GOALS

1. _____

2. _____

3. _____

4. _____

5. _____

6. _____

7. _____

8. _____

9. _____

10. _____

Now, write down actions you can take to reach your goals. These should be small, specific steps that align with your values. For example:

- ✧ Respect - make an effort to listen more in conversations.
- ✧ Success - break your big goal into smaller tasks and tackle them one by one.
- ✧ Gratitude - start a gratitude journal and list three things you're thankful for each day.
- ✧ Honesty - practice expressing your thoughts clearly, even when it's difficult.
- ✧ Kindness - offer help to someone in need or do something nice for a friend or stranger.

ACTIONS

1. _____
_____

2. _____
_____

3. _____
_____

4. _____
_____

5. _____
_____

6. _____
_____

7. _____
_____

8. _____
_____

9. _____
_____

10. _____

_____

It is important to answer this truthfully as it can help you align your actions with your beliefs and values. In most cases, the answer is straightforward. You either take some action that aligns with these values, or you don't. The exercise is to create goals that align with what you believe in. The action should match your value. If it doesn't, think about what you need to change in order for that to happen. Write that down, and then remind yourself that you have a goal every time your mind feels like it starts to go down a rabbit hole.

What Did You Learn in This Chapter?

This is a chapter that only opened the doors for you toward a whole different world. Out of everything you've read, here is a summary of what you learned in part 1:

✧ The concept of mindfulness.

✧ The power and the characteristics of the wise mind.

✧ The importance of what skills – observing, describing, and participating.

✧ The importance of the how skills – non-judgmentally, one-mindfully, and effectively.

As we close the part on mindfulness, we embark on an adventure – and right into the second part! There, we are going to discuss everything connected to distress tolerance – what it is, learning how to refine it – everything. So, turn the page – and let's discover some wonderful new things together!

Part 2

DISTRESS TOLERANCE

"The real man smiles in trouble, gathers strength from distress, and grows brave by reflection."

– Thomas Paine

In the first part of this book, we began by highlighting mindfulness. I did mention that mindfulness will be the foundation upon which you will build yourself up. So, this second part is about something that is closely connected to the topic of mindfulness. It is a sort of an extension of mindfulness.

Let's start from the very beginning. If you have never heard or thought about it until today, we will discuss distress – and everything connected to it. Later on, as the chapter unravels, we will also include much more information linked to it. All of this will help you regulate your emotions and increase your interpersonal effectiveness.

What Is Distress Tolerance?

Have you ever asked yourself if you are a person that gets agitated quickly? I mean, you are a teenager, so this is kind of "a given". But how do you perceive yourself? Considering we have removed the factor that you are in your teen years?

Distress tolerance is your ability to manage perceived emotional distress. It includes making it through an emotional episode without worsening the situation. People who are dealing with low distress tolerance may become a little overwhelmed whenever they come face to face with a stressful situation. Sometimes, when this happens, they may even turn to a very unhealthy or destructive outlet that would help them cope with it.

But the thing is – everyone experiences stress every once in a while. You've probably found yourself experiencing stress, too. You can experience stress over everything – a fight at home, bad grades, lost romantic interest, etc. No matter how small or large this stress is, it can affect your ability to manage that particular situation. Sometimes, you can notice how it's more difficult for you to manage strong negative emotions such as guilt, anxiety, fear, shame, anger, and sadness. The stronger the emotion is, the more difficult it is to control it.

Poor distress tolerance can be a very challenging thing. The first thing you need to do in this situation is to identify the emotions you're experiencing. However, as a teenager who doesn't have that much experience on the topic, identifying such strong emotions may be terrifying. The relief you may get from a self-destructive measure is only a short-term one. The truth is that every distressing emotion can make matters worse and pile up feelings of guilt and shame, ultimately leading to you being even more upset.

Thankfully, there is some good news behind all this! After all, that's why we're here. There are many techniques we can work on together to help you cope with the intense emotions you have. These healthy distress tolerance outlets are perfect! With their assistance, you can create a long-term outlook on dealing with every challenging thing in your life.

Increasing your distress tolerance can be an effective way to help yourself regulate your impulsivity and anger. This can come with many other benefits, ultimately leading to you living a calmer, happier, and more serene life.

Before we go into the techniques to work on, let's look at the factors a bit. Oftentimes, you need to realize that what you are feeling is okay, but it has not been within your control because you were not aware that such a background exists with emotions in the first place.

For example, there may be biological influences on distress tolerance. The temperament you have may just be the indicator of the level of difficulty you're met with each time you face a challenging situation.

Another example is distorted beliefs. Suppose you are intolerant when it comes to challenges. In that case, you may find yourself thinking you're always upset about something, that you will never feel better, and that everything is terrible, or you hate everyone – or everyone hates you. These types of thinking patterns can make it more challenging for you to come up with upsetting events. While these are automatic thoughts, they often result in avoidance, withdrawal, and even self-harm.

I know that, while reading this, you already felt a little bit distressed, but don't worry. The reason why we go deeper into this subject together is to help you come out the other side better, stronger, and happier. With that in mind, let's move on to the distress tolerance techniques.

Distraction

The first one is distraction. This can be a very easy way to take action and thus increase your distress tolerance level. It usually includes various methods that can help you take your mind off of things. The different methods can be as follows:

- ✧ Distract yourself by doing something you like – when times get tough, turn your attention to something you really like to do. It can be anything, as long as it is an activity that will help you become fully present in the moment.

- ✧ Distract yourself by focusing your attention on someone else – it is about realizing that sometimes, more than just one person goes through a difficult period. Depending on your situation, there will often be other people involved. Some of the distractions you can indulge in include people watching (sitting outside on a bench and quietly observing people), calling someone (a friend or a relative, just to check on them, and see how they are), or going outside and physically meeting someone.

- ✧ Distract yourself by doing chores – probably the most effective (and used) approach of all is distracting yourself by throwing yourself into work. There is a certain satisfaction in completing a task, something you cannot feel with anything else. So, when you're facing a difficult situation, it is time to find all the things you've put on the back burner and complete them. The chores can be anything – from rearranging your clothes to doing your dishes, redecorating – anything that will make you feel like you are doing something important – because you are.

While we discuss these simple yet effective distraction methods, it is important to realize that they are here not only to help you cope but to help you in the long run as well. Consider utilizing them whenever you feel stuck or have a strong sense of negative emotions washing over you. I must warn you – it will be challenging in the beginning! You may not be able to focus on one thing at a time or anything because you still haven't completely succeeded in controlling your emotions, but don't worry! Practice makes it perfect, and the sooner you start, the better!

And while we are on the topic of practicing, it is time to move on to the next exercise.

EXERCISE 11
IDENTIFYING HEALTHY AND UNHEALTHY DISTRACTIONS

This one is connected to how you perceive things as good and bad. We already learned that distractions are coping mechanisms – but some can have a positive effect, while others can negatively influence your overall life. In this exercise, I am going to help you differentiate between them and pay close attention to what is good and what is bad.

Take out a pen and paper, or use the worksheet below, and imagine a scenario where you are challenged in a certain way. You've faced a difficult situation, and now you need to know how to healthily cope with it. But also, before you start writing things down, consider everything you've read so far in this chapter.

Now begin – divide your piece of paper by drawing a vertical line down the middle of it. On the left side, write healthy; on the right, write unhealthy distractions. Keep that scenario in your mind. It may even help more if you have multiple scenarios or past events just to compare your behavior. In some cases, you may have turned to things such as sleeping a lot, avoiding the issue, shutting down, overeating (or not eating enough), and so on. These are all the unhealthy distractions you've participated in – so you can put them in the right section. Now think about all the cases where you faced the issue at hand; be understanding, indulge in physical activity, or talk to someone about it. All of these things are healthy distractions, and they can actually help you cope.

Healthy Distractions

Unhealthy Distractions

_____

_____

_____

_____

_____

_____

_____

_____

_____

_____

_____

_____

_____

_____

_____

_____

_____

_____

_____

_____

_____

_____

_____

_____

_____

_____

_____

_____

Even though these might not have necessarily been the things you wrote down, you get the idea. To know which of all the responses should go in the left and which ones should be in the right section, think about this – there is a certain result that comes with every little thing we do. This is an essential thing to remember when it comes to distractions. The result may be you end up feeling better – or worse. That's how you know what is healthy and what is an unhealthy way to cope with things. Out of all the things that crossed your mind, how many of them have truly made you feel calm and better? Focus on them because these are the good things, the productive distractions.

Radical Acceptance

Has it ever happened to you to face a situation that is so difficult you thought it would be impossible to accept it? Maybe you had a falling out with your best friend, or a very bad grade, or a fight with your parents. This can be anything that has made you feel like everything around you is falling apart, and you can't really deal with it. This is where the second skill comes in handy – and it is radical acceptance.

Sometimes, trying to cut out all the unnecessary drama in life is advisable. It is also advisable to accept a situation as it is. After all, there is a lot of relief behind that, so why not try it? Things are not in your control anyway, and there is no harm in letting go. By doing this, you practice radical acceptance.

Think of it this way – you are not accepting the pain or approving of it in any way. On the contrary, you simply allow yourself to focus on what is in your control and what you can do. It is all about creating a shift in your energy. Rather than preparing for war and leading with your emotions, you start to plan your next move and do that with a calm and clear mind.

You should accept radical acceptance if you're willing to go through life's challenges stronger than ever. As a part of DBT, it is a technique that includes embracing the present moment. The situations you may find yourself in the middle of during your life can be highly challenging. Some of them may even be borderline unbearable. Radical acceptance comes into place when things seem almost impossible. I'm talking about situations where most people would run from. Radical acceptance means facing all these challenges without trying to avoid or change them.

So, how does radical acceptance function?

The thing you need to realize here is that it is not about acceptance. You cannot just be okay with a situation that is obviously far from optimal, right? Radical acceptance is just acknowledging a situation – as it is, without any judgment. At that moment, you stop fighting reality. I know that this is a lot easier to read about than to do in actual life, but the more of it you accept, the more resilient you become. This technique is created to help you build some tolerance against distress. Because this is where the real magic happens, radically accepting reality, with all its painful parts, can help you open the door to personal transformation and growth.

Radical acceptance comes with many benefits. All you need to do is truly commit to it. The few reasons why you are developing this as a skill, are to start cultivating self-compassion, increase your tolerance to distress, to no longer fight what cannot be changed, to improve your ability to cope and solve issues effectively, to stay away from harsh judgment, and deepen your capacity to accept things in all areas of your life. Picture radical acceptance as a threshold you need to cross to get to the other side happier. But, in order to achieve this, you will need to practice it. I have prepared a couple of exercises for you to try. But before that, let's talk a little about how to practice radical acceptance.

All of this may seem simple in theory, but it can be quite challenging in practice. But, to master it, you still need to practice it. To do that, here are a few steps I always like to incorporate. These steps have helped many other people as well as myself, so I am sharing them with you so that after much practice, they can become your "second nature".

- ✧ You may discover you are constantly fighting against your reality (complaining or wishing that everything was different).
- ✧ Then, you start acknowledging what reality is, even if you don't really like it. You notice that you can't change anything about the situation.
- ✧ You make the choice to accept the situation as it is and breathe into the discomfort of it all.
- ✧ You start embracing self-compassion. There are many painful emotions as you go through the process, but you suddenly realize that beating yourself up about it will only make things worse, not better.
- ✧ Finally, you start to shift your focus. At that exact moment, you ask yourself what the next thing you can do to be effective and take better care of yourself is.

The trick with radical acceptance is that you need to start small and know how to cope properly. The change process is long, so you also need to be compassionate and patient with yourself. If you need some more time to master this – take the time. Don't put pressure on yourself. Go through the exercises I have prepared for you and guide yourself toward the new realm of acceptance and understanding.

EXERCISE 12
ACCEPTING DIFFICULT EMOTIONS

This exercise is about embracing change and accepting the things that cannot be changed. Radical acceptance is not always easy, but that doesn't mean you can't incorporate it into your life – starting today. Think about it this way – there are a few statements you can say whenever you are faced with a challenging situation. After all, the most difficult part of radical acceptance is to go through and feel the emotions, no matter how hard it is.

Take a pen and paper, or use the worksheet below, and sit down. Think of a situation where you felt like your entire world was turned upside down. Think of the most difficult situation you've ever been in and the feelings that you have. If you haven't gone through the process, you might still notice the negative emotions surfacing. Accepting difficult emotions is about knowing how to handle them. Now, you're going to start handling them by using coping statements.

To get you started on this, here are a few examples:

✧ I am able to accept the present moment as it is.

✧ I know I will get through this no matter what.

✧ I will survive, and this feeling will pass.

✧ I can't change what happened in the past, but I can learn to let go and focus on the present.

✧ Fighting my negative emotions only makes them stronger. I now allow them to wash over me and pass.

✧ I can choose to create my own path despite the negative history.

✧ I don't need to judge, just to take the appropriate action toward the future.

✦ I can get through all the complex emotions, even though they seem like the most difficult thing to do at the present moment.

You can either use these, create your own coping statements that would work best for you, or make a mix of both. Some of the examples you can take from your own experience include:

✦ My fallout with my friend does not define me as a person.

✦ When I look in the mirror, I choose to see the good.

✦ My bad grade does not mean that I will fail at everything.

✦ I love myself no matter what.

✦ My romantic interest may not be interested in me anymore, and that's okay.

Either way, these can be an excellent reminder that tomorrow will be better than today and that you already have all the tools to accept difficult emotions.

Situation: _____

Coping Statement: _____

_____

_____

Situation: _____

Coping Statement: _____

_____

_____

Situation: _____

Coping Statement: _____

_____

_____

_____

Situation: _____

Coping Statement: _____

_____

_____

_____

Situation: _____

Coping Statement: _____

_____

_____

_____

Situation: _____

Coping Statement: _____

_____

_____

_____

Situation: _____

Coping Statement: _____

_____

_____

_____

Situation: _____

Coping Statement: _____

_____

_____

_____

Situation: _____

Coping Statement: _____

_____

_____

_____

Situation: _____

Coping Statement: _____

_____

_____

_____

Situation: _____

Coping Statement: _____

_____

_____

_____

Situation: _____

Coping Statement: _____

_____

_____

_____

Situation: _____

Coping Statement: _____

_____

_____

_____

Situation: _____

Coping Statement: _____

_____

_____

_____

EXERCISE 13
DIFFICULT SITUATIONS

As you can realize, radical acceptance is a skill that gets better the more you practice it. In this exercise, together, we are learning how to cope with difficult situations. To improve your engagement in radical acceptance, you need to know how to take the proper steps in a difficult situation. Here are the steps – all you need to do is memorize them and try them out next time you come face to face with an almost impossible situation.

1. Think about resistance. Certain cases act like triggers; notice them. It is only in those situations that you cannot accept something.

2. When something difficult happens, remind yourself that you cannot change the situation.

3. Then, remind yourself that things are absolutely out of your control.

4. Think about what would happen if you started to accept the situation as it is. Imagine what it would be like to receive the problem.

5. Suppose it is not possible to do that. In that case, you can always utilize some relaxation strategies such as journalling, self-reflection, and mindfulness practices to help you understand your emotions and what you're going through.

6. Allow yourself to feel safe in your skin and feel all the emotions.

7. Observe what kind of an effect they have on your body. Does your chest feel tight? Do you need to breathe deeply? Is there any pain?

8. Always remember that life is still worthwhile, even with a lot of pain in it.

9. Practice this acceptance process whenever you feel like you have some issues with a particular situation.

These magnificent steps can help you stop thinking about how things could have been and help you start thinking about the things that are at the moment. These steps will help you stay present. To know when these steps are best used, here are a few example situations for you. These include situations that you might have already been in by now. If not, they will give you a perfect starting point so you can brainstorm some situations that actually have happened to you. As you read them, think about something similar happening to you. You can also use the lines below to make some notes.

- ✧ When you have an argument with a friend at school, and you feel a lot of emotions.
- ✧ When you want to explain something to someone, and it looks as if they don't understand you - and you get frustrated about it.
- ✧ When something you see happening reminds you of a certain situation that happened to you.
- ✧ When it looks like you may need some help to repair something.
- ✧ When you come face to face with a challenge.

_____

_____

_____

_____

_____

_____

_____

_____

_____

_____

_____

_____

_____

_____

_____

_____

_____

_____

_____

_____

_____

_____

_____

_____

_____

Self-Soothing

In life, you're always going to face some ups and downs. There will be plenty of moments of happiness, but also there will be some tough times too. Before I go into the following technique, this is a gentle reminder for you – you live in a very fast-paced world. As humans, we are not created to endure as much as we do. So, when you're feeling emotionally distressed, just keep in mind that it is okay.

That leads me to the topic of self-soothing. DBT is designed in such a way to help you navigate tough situations with so much ease. It teaches you how to be constructive and deal with every situation healthily. Out of all the tools and techniques we're going to cover in this book together, this one is both the most effective and the most challenging. The self-soothing means using all the senses you have to bring calmness into your existence. It comes with a set of sensory strategies (the two exercises in this section will help you with that), so let's get started.

The interesting thing about self-soothing is that it is connected to the distress tolerance. When you are in the middle of a situation that causes some intense emotions, the one helpful thing is to try to relax in the moment using your senses. In these moments, self-soothing can help a lot because you feel highly overwhelmed, and you need a pleasant sensation to calm down. Self-soothing skills focus on the five senses of taste, hearing, smell, sight, and touch. In those moments when you feel incredibly distressed, you might find it difficult to navigate through this and get back to your senses. However, you can always rely on self-soothing skills.

Get ready to go through some trial and error while you practice this. Still, in the end, you will experience the ultimate stress relief from it. The goal here is to practice this for as long as you need until you are confident you can turn to them whenever you need them.

Since it is about engaging the five senses, let's take a look at each of those senses individually, shall we? Below, I am sharing some suggestions with you. These can be your starting point as you go through your soothing journey.

- ✧ Let's start with sight. Whenever you feel distressed, turn to something that means a lot to you – for example, take a look at a picture of your partner (if you already have one), your family, or your pet – as long as you feel the love overflowing you while you look at it.

- ✧ Move on to the sound. In a stressful situation, all people, especially teenagers, have found sound to be the most soothing thing they can turn to. Put on some music and allow the feeling of calmness to wash over you.

- ✧ Taste something. A simple thing such as chewing your favorite gum can help you recenter and feel much better instantly. Your favorite meal may just help you bring yourself back to yourself again.

- ✧ Try using your smell. Another incredible thing about different scents is that they remind us of different things. To calm yourself down at a given moment, you can always turn to your favorite perfume, lotion, or spray. There is a certain mindfulness to smelling something that reminds you of good times.

- ✧ The final one is touch. A soft blanket, a favorite toy, or your most comfortable clothes – touching something that feels comfortable is one of the best ways to calm down in a stressful situation.

Self-soothing as a concept seems relatively straightforward, but when the time comes for you to actually utilize it, it may feel like it's a little more than just challenging. That's why I've created two excellent exercises where you can get the most out of this skill.

EXERCISE 14
RELAXATION

There is a little bit of science behind the relaxation exercise, specifically because it is paired with muscle relaxation. Allow me to explain this a little more. Lay down, or sit down comfortably in a chair, and completely relax your entire body. Now, to fully relax your muscles, try to breathe in and out deeply and slowly, and slow down your heart rate with it, too.

Focus on one group of muscles and try to tighten them. Hold for a few seconds, and then relax. Allow them to rest for a few seconds before doing that again. Each time you tighten and relax your muscles, you slowly release the tension. Go into detail, and as you inhale and exhale through the process, feel your muscles relaxing, one at a time. Once you notice that one group of muscles is relaxed (for example your arms), you can move on to the next group of muscles and so on. As soon as you know it, your entire body will feel completely relaxed.

EXERCISE 15
BUILDING A SELF-SOOTHE KIT

Before I moved on to the exercises, I mentioned the five senses – touch, sight, hearing, smell, and taste. This exercise can help you combine them in order to create a self-soothing kit that is a perfect fit for you. Let's put the words into action!

Take a pen and a piece of paper (or use the worksheet below), and on one side, write all the five senses. Now, with the help of the examples I presented above, start to brainstorm. Dedicate some time to each sense and think about what calms you down. Try writing down a few things next to each sense. For example:

Sound – the sound of waves crashing on the shore, the sound of my favorite playlist, etc.

As soon as you're done writing this and brainstorming about each sense, take a look at what you've written. Right now, you have, in your hands, your own self-soothing kit. It is designed by you, for you, and as long as you are completely honest while writing it, this can help you every time you feel distressed. Think of this as your first-aid kit. Whenever you find yourself in a challenging situation, simply go back to it, open it up, and use all the power that is placed inside of it.

Sight _____

_____

_____

_____

Sound _____

_____

_____

_____

Taste _____

_____

_____

_____

Smell _____

_____

_____

_____

Touch _____

_____

_____

_____

Pros and Cons

Moving on to the pros and cons. I know the thought that crossed your mind right now – the pros and cons are relatively easy to do, and you already know what they are. But not in DBT terms. The pros and cons of DBT are very different from the mainstream pros and cons we all know. *The way DBT views pros and cons is by focusing on tolerating vs. not tolerating or coping vs. not coping.* In other words, pros and cons in a distressing situation using DBT means looking at all the consequences of all the potential actions you may take.

Since the exercise here would be a little bit larger, we can move on to it together. Study the method and discover how to make the most of this DBT skill.

EXERCISE 16
PROS AND CONS WORKSHEET

The best way for me to describe this skill is by putting it in motion. Picture a difficult situation – it can be something you make up as you go or a past situation that stuck with you. It can be anything – a challenge at home, school, or friends. Now, think about your initial response to that situation. Is it filled with outbursts, with a lot of emotions, and with a response that you could barely control? This is something we're trying to change through this exercise.

Write down the initial response that automatically came to your mind. Now, it is time to create the pros and cons worksheet. Divide your piece of paper into two sections and write the pros in one and the cons in the other section. You can also use the worksheet below.

Now, when you write the pros and cons of this specific situation, you will do that by utilizing DBT. Answer these questions:

- ✧ How can you step out of this situation with success?
- ✧ Can you get what you want out of it?
- ✧ Are you used to being in distress?
- ✧ What would happen if you spoke up?
- ✧ How can you tweak the initial response to get better results?

Write all the answers down and separate them into the cons or the pros section. As you look at the piece of paper with all the emotional and logical things included, you end up realizing that there may be more to the story (taking a look at things from the other side's perspective) and that you can always choose what you act on (emotions, logic, or both).

Here are a few example situations for you:

1. You have a fight over different opinions with a friend.
2. You get scolded by your parents for something you did or didn't do.
3. You failed to deliver a project at school.
4. You bailed on your friends without explanation.
5. You had a fight with your sibling.

Let's take one of these situations as an example for our answers. For example - failing to deliver a project at school. How can you respond to that? Let's take a look at a few example answers:

1. You may come up with a constructive answer that shows the reality of the situation.
2. You may panic and start crying.
3. You may communicate with your teacher and ask them if you could finish the project and deliver it at a later date.
4. You may blame someone else for you not being able to complete the project on time.
5. You may break down completely and argue with your teacher.

Now, think of the consequences of each one of these answers. For some answers, the consequences are good, and for some, they are bad. You can easily categorize them. To make the most out of every situation in the long run, you need to respond calmly and honestly. That way, you can act on both logic and emotion.

Situation: _____

Initial Response: _____

_____

Pros:

_____   Cons:

_____   _____

_____   _____

_____   _____

_____   _____

_____   _____

                                      _____

Situation: _____

Initial Response: _____

_____

Pros:

_____   Cons:

_____   _____

_____   _____

_____   _____

_____   _____

_____   _____

                                      _____

Situation: _____

Initial Response: _____

_____

Pros: Cons:

_____   _____

_____   _____

_____   _____

_____   _____

_____   _____

_____   _____

Situation: _____

Initial Response: _____

_____

Pros: Cons:

_____   _____

_____   _____

_____   _____

_____   _____

_____   _____

Situation: _____

Initial Response: _____

_____

Pros:

_____

_____

_____

_____

_____

_____

Cons:

_____

_____

_____

_____

_____

_____

Situation: _____

Initial Response: _____

_____

Pros:

_____

_____

_____

_____

_____

_____

Cons:

_____

_____

_____

_____

_____

_____

Situation: _____

Initial Response: _____

_____

Pros: Cons:

_____   _____

_____   _____

_____   _____

_____   _____

_____   _____

_____   _____

Situation: _____

Initial Response: _____

_____

Pros: Cons:

_____   _____

_____   _____

_____   _____

_____   _____

_____   _____

_____   _____

Situation: _____

Initial Response: _____

_____

Pros:

_____   Cons:

_____   _____

_____   _____

_____   _____

_____   _____

_____   _____

Situation: _____

Initial Response: _____

_____

Pros: Cons:

_____   _____

_____   _____

_____   _____

_____   _____

_____   _____

What Did You Learn From This Chapter?

As we slowly close this chapter, this is the part where we reflect upon everything we've discovered together so far. While your journey is just getting started, you have done an amazing job up to this point. Let's see what you can take away from this part with you:

- ✧ What is distress tolerance, and how to increase it.
- ✧ Distraction as a powerful distress tolerance technique – and how you can utilize it.
- ✧ Radical acceptance – one of the pillars of DBT and a skill that can serve you the most.
- ✧ How to come to terms with difficult situations by incorporating the self-soothing skills – what are they, how powerful are they, and how easy it is to use them.
- ✧ The magnificence of making a pros and cons worksheet – they are very different from the pros and cons you're used to.

As the mind becomes stronger and healthier, so does the body. Until now, we have focused on bringing together all aspects of DBT and utilizing them in your mind. In the following section, we will shift our focus and gain a whole new perspective on things. Turn the page and start the next chapter – because it is all about properly dealing with your emotions!

Part 3

EMOTIONAL REGULATION

*"I don't want to be at the mercy of my
emotions. I want to use them, to enjoy them,
and to dominate them."*

– Oscar Wilde

I t is always important to keep your emotions in check. As you can see from what you read so far, you can't really shut them out. Emotions are important, and they are a healthy way to express yourself. But when is it "enough" of emotions? Until now, we have talked about matters of the mind, but now we get to talk about matters of the soul.

You communicate with yourself and with other people through emotions. It is an excellent way to create relationships and approach situations. But as a teenager, you may not always know how to control your emotions. Sometimes, they come in large shipments, and you don't know what to do with them all. So, you unload them. You unload them on yourself, and on the people around you. At the moment, while you're doing that, it even feels like a storm is happening inside of you. But once the moment has passed, you look at things differently, from another (calmer) perspective, and you may notice that you've created chaos.

It is just as challenging to control your emotions as it is challenging to control your thoughts. That's why, in this part, you will uncover everything you need to know about your emotions. I will start from the very beginning, so get ready – because it is quite an interesting process to go through!

What Is Emotional Regulation?

Emotional regulation means taking action to alter the intensity of any emotional experience. Many of you may think that this is a way to hide and suppress your emotions when it cannot be farther from it. Emotional regulation means having the ability to have full control over your emotions through many approaches.

As you go through your life, you will notice that some people are better at regulating their emotions. These people seem to have a higher emotional intelligence, and it may seem like they are fully aware of their experiences within and the experiences of those around them. These people seem naturally calm.

While this is true – these people are calm – they still experience a fair share of negative emotions. They have just managed to regulate their emotions properly. Emotional regulation is not something you have or don't have – it's something you improve and master over time. In life, you will face many challenges and difficulties, which can take their toll on your physical and mental health.

This is why emotional regulation is so important. Slowly, you are reaching the stage of adulthood, and as an adult, you are expected to regulate your emotions that fit with the "socially acceptable way of handling them". It is known that when emotions get the best of us, sometimes they lead to issues.

The thing is, there are many things that can influence emotional regulation. Every stressful situation you've ever had to deal with provoked powerful emotions from within. I have mentioned this a few times throughout the chapters.

Now, you are aware that you may hurt relationships by not taking charge of your emotions. It is the kind of emotional volatility that can make a change for the worse. You may end up saying or doing things you never meant to do in the first place.

Other than having an overall negative impact on any relationship, feeling overwhelmed can cause unnecessary struggles and suffering. If you don't start dealing with it, then you will have to deal with a lifetime of not having new opportunities and experiences.

It is all about maintaining a positive reaction - that's what this chapter will delve into. The thing we're learning here is how to properly respond to a challenging situation, and together, we are going to cover a few important things.

First, we're going to start with opposite action, and a few exercises that can help you develop it. Then, we are going to move to learning how to focus on the positive. Finally, we are going to focus on ourselves, and our physical health as well.

Opposite Action

Putting those words into action is something you will start doing now! It is time to fully control your emotions and discover the power of emotional regulation! Opposite action will teach you how to do just that!

When all emotions are activated, they make us respond in a certain way. It seems like we are almost pre-programmed to do that with all of them. The opposite action is a skill that can help you respond completely the opposite of how you normally would. This is how you get ready to act and take control over yourself. Of course, this means focusing on the negative emotions only whenever you want to take the opposite action.

That leads me to the first exercise of this part. Here it is below.

EXERCISE 17
RESPONDING OPPOSITE TO INTENSE EMOTIONS

It is all about learning how to recognize and deal with your emotions. Yes, it will take a lot of practice to make this happen, but this exercise is an excellent starting point. Once combined with the other ones from this chapter, they bring together all the aspects of emotional regulation you need to know and practice.

For this exercise, think of five emotions you feel most of the time. Keep in mind that they should be negative emotions. Write them down on a piece of paper, or on the worksheet below, and write how they make you act. Now, after you're done with that, write down the opposite reactions of these emotions. It is a kind of role-playing where you think of the opposite reaction to your intense emotions. For example:

When you feel shame, you have the need to hide.

But the opposite of shame is keeping your head up and facing anything head-on.

When you feel depressed, you feel like you want to curl up and stay away from the world.

But the opposite of that is going out, getting active, and staying in touch with everything and everyone.

When you feel anger, you want to attack or defend yourself.

But the opposite is to show concern and kindness – or simply walk away.

Create this list and stick to it – especially if you want the negative emotions to go away and for you to feel less uncomfortable. This is the perfect skill – along with the belief you hold within that this kind of exercise will work!

Emotion: _____

Action: _____

_____

Opposite Action: _____

_____

Emotion: _____

Action: _____

_____

Opposite Action: _____

_____

Emotion: _____

Action: _____

_____

Opposite Action: _____

_____

Emotion: _____

Action: _____

_____

Opposite Action: _____

_____

Emotion: _____

Action: _____

_____

Opposite Action: _____

_____

Focusing on the Facts and Problem-Solving

Problem-solving seems like a relatively easy thing to do. Once you are met with an issue, you need to figure out the best course of action and then proceed to resolve it. The thing is, while it all sounds good "on paper", it's not that easy to do in life. Sometimes, you may find yourself in situations where there isn't really a way out – at least, that's how it seems in the beginning. I am here to tell you that problem-solving, as a technique, cannot truly exist if it is not connected with the former one – and that is focusing on the facts. Fact-checking and problem-solving skills as a part of DBT are essential and should be looked into immediately.

The main goal of this skill is to help you manage and regulate your emotional response by looking at the facts and the facts only. It is about examining the facts supporting your feelings, assumptions, and thoughts. This process can help you differentiate between judgments and interpretations. And if you haven't been aware of it by now – these two can often distort emotions. Focusing on the facts as a DBT skill can help you both with emotional regulation and with distress tolerance. You will see, once you finish this book, that all of the skills and techniques you will uncover here are connected.

Now, let's do some work! Here are the steps you need to take in order to check the facts when it comes to DBT:

✧ Identify the emotion. Look within yourself to find out what you are feeling and why you are feeling that particular emotion.

✧ Identify the event next. What happened to you that triggered the emotion you're dealing with at the moment? Can you pinpoint that?

✧ Clarify your thoughts. A certain chain of thoughts started roaming around your mind as you felt those emotions. Identify those thoughts –they could definitely be connected to a belief you hold on to.

✧ Start looking at the facts – and checking them. Evaluate the situation and whether the emotion and intensity match the facts of your situation.

✧ Create a new response. After you look at the emotions and the facts, it is time for you to check if they align. If they don't (which will probably be the case), you need to change your emotional reaction and create one that suits the facts better.

As you can see, this is the perfect DBT skill for a teenager – because you are the ones who struggle with emotions the most! Also, you are the ones who have the most difficulty distinguishing between the reality of a situation and your thoughts. Fact-checking means improving your emotional intelligence. Fact-checking can help you draft healthier responses to any kind of situation.

And, if you think that this is not something that's created for you – think again. This DBT skill can be used by anyone who needs some assistance managing their feelings, emotional responses, negative thoughts, or anything else. While this is an incredibly powerful tool for adults who want to improve their emotional intelligence, teenagers can benefit from it in the same way. After using this skill for a while, you will notice that you can resolve conflicts better, you can improve your overall well-being and enhance your mental strength. While I am on the topic of how this skill can help, why not look at all the benefits that come from it? Here, I am sharing some of the best ones with you, hoping to get you practicing this skill as soon as possible!

- ✧ Your emotional intelligence will improve. As a skill, fact-checking can help you better understand your emotions and the triggers behind them, thus resulting in improved self-awareness on an emotional level.

- ✧ You will stop reacting as impulsively. Granted, your parents probably say this will happen to you once you step out of the teenage era and into adulthood, but this is not always the case. It is all about analyzing if the emotions fit the facts. Doing this can help you reduce any overreactions and emotional responses that are not adequate for the situation you're dealing with.

- ✧ You will improve your problem-solving skills. A clever approach once means a clever approach again. After some time, this kind of clever approach will help you get a clearer scope of the situation and will give you the assistance to make rational decisions and seek effective solutions.

- ✧ You will improve your relationships with the people around you. Once you have a better understanding of your emotions, you will lead not only with your mind but also with empathy. As you understand that, your connections with the people around you will grow stronger and better.

- ✧ You will enjoy improved mental health. Nowadays, it seems like mental health is a topic often communicated among people – and for a good reason. By implementing this approach, you can strengthen your overall mental health and maintain it at an optimal level.

- ✧ Your self-confidence will skyrocket! Yes, I do mean this! When you do good, you see good, and you are good, you will end up feeling good! Gaining control over your emotions will lead to increased self-esteem and much more confidence when you handle a challenging situation in your life.

So, you see, the sole act of focusing on the facts will help you go a long way, especially because it will help you become a little more rational and turn to that corner of your mind that we mentioned earlier – the wise mind. Speaking of which, let's move on to the exercises connected to the fact-checking aspect of DBT.

EXERCISE 18
CHALLENGE IRRATIONAL THOUGHTS

When you're focusing on the facts, it means that you are challenging everything you believe in. It's true – this is when your entire belief system is being broken down. So, in order to start that up, you will need to challenge every irrational thought that goes through your mind. Let's talk about checking the facts.

Sit down and think of a situation where you had arrangements with people, and you've been looking forward to spending time with these people. Now, imagine that, in that particular situation, the people you were supposed to meet cancelled on you at the last moment. Now, think about how that would make you feel. Would you feel nervous, sad, or angry? Or maybe some other feeling you associate with when facing such an event? As soon as the emotions surface, it is time for you to do that fact-checking. Here are the steps you're going to take.

1. Identify the emotion first. For example, in this case, you might feel very angry.

2. Identify what caused you to feel that way. The cancelation of plans.

3. Start describing the event. How did you feel when you initially heard that? What was the first thing that crossed your mind? Did you start thinking that they don't appreciate your time, or they're just pulling your chain, or they don't care about you, and they never have?

4. Start with your interpretation. Go deeper into what you thought and felt. Why does this make you feel this way? Go deeper and find the reason.

5. Now check the facts. Has this been the first time these people have cancelled on you? Or maybe you've cancelled them a few times before, and they seemed fine with it? Did they apologize to you?

6. Come out with the facts. After you start rationalizing a little bit, things will easily start to put themselves into perspective. It is completely understandable to feel annoyed, disappointed, or even sad about the entire new situation, but the situation is really not that important to be that angry about it. You slowly start to realize that the extreme response you have does not match the severity of the situation – especially if there is a reasonable explanation behind it.

7. Start formulating a new response. How would you react the next time such a situation happens to you? Would you know how to properly formulate your response? Remember that while it is always okay to feel slightly disappointed, that is not an excuse to blow the situation out of proportion. It is all about checking the facts and then comparing them to your current emotions, thoughts, and feelings.

This exercise of checking the facts will help you rationalize and will help you calm yourself down every time you feel like a strong surge of emotions is coming to the surface. Here are a few situations when you can use this:

1. Whenever you feel anxiety about a social event.
2. When you are having an argument with a friend (or just had one).
3. When a crush rejects you.
4. Whenever you feel like your parents are criticizing you a lot.
5. Whenever you fail an exam.

Emotion: _____

Reason for the Emotion: _____

Describe the Event: _____

_____

_____

_____

Go Deeper: _____

_____

_____

_____

Facts: _____

_____

_____

_____

Your New Response: _____

_____

_____

_____

_____

Emotion: _____

Reason for the Emotion: _____

Describe the Event: _____

_____

_____

_____

Go Deeper: _____

_____

_____

_____

Facts: _____

_____

_____

_____

Your New Response: _____

_____

_____

_____

_____

Emotion: _____

Reason for the Emotion: _____

Describe the Event: _____

_____

_____

_____

Go Deeper: _____

_____

_____

_____

Facts: _____

_____

_____

_____

Your New Response: _____

_____

_____

_____

_____

Emotion: _____

Reason for the Emotion: _____

Describe the Event: _____

_____

_____

_____

Go Deeper: _____

_____

_____

_____

Facts: _____

_____

_____

_____

Your New Response: _____

_____

_____

_____

_____

Emotion: _____

Reason for the Emotion: _____

Describe the Event: _____

_____

_____

_____

Go Deeper: _____

_____

_____

_____

Facts: _____

_____

_____

_____

Your New Response: _____

_____

_____

_____

_____

EXERCISE 19
PROBLEM-SOLVING TECHNIQUES

The second exercise is connected to the aspect of problem-solving. The truth is that how you feel about a problem is more important than the actual problem. This is a saying you will learn to be true after this exercise. Sometimes, when you come face to face with a certain situation, you may feel insecure and unable to solve the issue at hand. Whenever you don't know how to proceed, you need to come back to this exercise. Well, this is not particularly an exercise but more of a set of techniques you can use to find yourself on the other side – with any situation or issue solved. Take failing an exam as an example:

1. Feel better about it – to start feeling better about failing the exam, you need to know how to regulate the emotions that surface. This may look like the opposite of what your gut is telling you, but it works. By exposing yourself to an uncomfortable situation, you may start to regulate your emotions better.

2. Tolerate it – here, I'm not talking about keeping quiet about the situation and turning a blind eye, but rather tolerating a situation you probably cannot change at the moment. This is the time to identify the problematic feelings and thoughts you have and try to bring yourself back to the present moment.

3. Stay in the current position – this may come as a shocker, mainly because we are working toward creating an attitude that will help you control your thoughts and emotions, but it is true. Sometimes, you may need a minute to deal with the shock of a certain situation. In this case, if the situation happens to be that serious or shocking, think of it this way – give it a minute. If you are not ready to rationalize and shift your perspective, then simply don't. Allow yourself the time you need to become calm and collected.

There are many people out there who believe that solving an issue can only have two outcomes. Sometimes, things are not as black and white as they seem, so whenever you feel like it, give yourself the time to calm down before you start exploring the right solution. Here are a few situations when you can make that happen:

1. Whenever you're coping with some friendship issues.
2. Whenever you feel like you have peer pressure.
3. Whenever school is starting to get to be too much for you.
4. When you have a conflict with a teacher.
5. When you struggle to properly manage your time.

Focus on the Positive

Easier said than done, right? But the thing is, increasing positive emotions is an essential part of creating an overall good life. Thankfully, there is an aspect of DBT that focuses just on that. Other than teaching you how to regulate and deal with negative emotions, it encourages you to focus on the positive ones. Focusing on the positive means providing you with more skills to help you manage emotions rather than the alternative – being managed by them. By doing this, you will even reduce your chances of negative emotions (and vulnerability caused by them) and will start building a positive emotional experience.

You need to understand here that you are not trying to put the positive emotions in place of all the negative feelings you've had. You are learning how to put them both in the same place. They should coexist, and as long as they do, it means you understand that sometimes the negative emotions will rule, and sometimes the positive emotions will rule – but no feeling is final.

That means building up the positive emotions does not mean you completely dismiss or remove the negative ones. You are simply expanding your experience. Now, in the beginning, this may be very challenging for you, especially if you have learned to focus on the negative for a long time. Thankfully, everything can be undone, and with the help of this DBT skill, so can the constant negative thinking.

To help you out, just so you can get started, there are a few ways to build positive emotions – both by including emotional experiences in your life. The first is focusing on short-term experiences, and the second is focusing on long-term experiences.

Let's try to differentiate them, shall we?

Short-term experiences are positive ones that are usually already a part of your everyday life. You may not give that much attention to them because they are something you do every day, but they make you feel good. This could be anything from walking in a park, watching your favorite TV show, talking to a friend, going for a run or a swim, or taking a bite out of your favorite meal. It is in these small things that we tend to find the true joy of life. When you do something you love, it fills you up with positive emotions. And no matter how difficult life may be for you, these positive emotions that come from short-term experiences mean a lot and can make a big change. The more you do them, the more positive energy you will create around you.

Long-term experiences are usually made up of positive things that have a long-lasting impact on the quality of your life. These are the things that are considered to make life worth living. For example, one of the things you can say to be the biggest positive long-term experience is your list of goals. Think about it – no matter what you do in life, you have a goal every day when you wake up. A driving force that gets you out of bed. For some people, this may be a combination of a few smaller goals, and for others, it may be one big goal that they have set their heart on. Your goals can be anything – from developing a new skill to learning how to craft something to moving to a different city or country, learning a new language, getting into college, getting the job of your dreams, etc. Here, the possibilities are endless. Think carefully about what would make your life more pleasant and happier. After you have the answers, turn those answers into goals and start working toward a better and brighter future.

Another thing that I'd like to include here is the relationships. Out of all the long-term experiences you may have in life, relationships are one of the most impactful things you can count on. Starting from a relationship with yourself and moving on to a relationship with the people around you, this is an important area of your life to work on. It can help you create a more positive future for yourself. You have probably seen this happening to some of your classmates at school – they have no issue developing any kind of relationships – whether they are personal or professional. This sometimes comes easy for some people, but for others, it can be a little challenging. Chances are, if you are reading this book, you are probably a part of the latter group – but that's okay! That's why I am here – to help you work through all the troubles you have and create a better version of yourself, as well as a happier life.

You can do both – reach out for new friendships and work on the existing ones. While both can be difficult at times, both are worth it. For example, working on the current relationships you have may be connected to anyone – from a friend to a sibling to a romantic interest. These are the people you spend a lot of time with. After working on maintaining a strong relationship with them, you can notice how your feelings improve. As this is a long-term commitment, you get a long-term positive experience out of it. Instead of letting your happiness depend on one person, try to cultivate many different relationships.

The second example is when you're trying to create a new relationship. This can be extremely difficult. The trick here is to find a place where you can do a joint activity with other people, such as dancing, bowling, singing, etc. Once you visit that place often, you will find yourself in the middle of a familiar crowd. Spark up a conversation with someone you think you can "click" with as a friend and make your way from there.

By this time, you should know what cultivating a positive emotion and experience means. In addition, we will turn to some fantastic exercises I've prepared for you to set you up for success!

EXERCISE 20
POSITIVE AFFIRMATIONS

When times get tough, it is all about focusing on the positive. For this exercise, you are going to do just that – try to focus on the positive. Only in this case, you will start with no one other than yourself. If you have not noticed this by now, all negative emotions come from a place of negative belief about ourselves. Once you realize that and try to shift your perspective, your environment and you will change as well. I have found that, with the power of positive affirmations, you can do anything you set your mind to – including changing your entire mindset from a negative to a positive one.

Look at yourself in the mirror as you do this. The first time you stand in front of your mirror is going to be a difficult one. Why? Because you will need to think of ten good things to say about yourself. These can be good things in terms of your mind, smile, energy–anything you can think of. Talking positively to yourself is an excellent way to start focusing on the positive. It can help you reprogram your mind and start looking for the good things everywhere you turn.

Now, while you stand in front of the mirror, talk about some things about yourself – some positive things. Say them out loud as if they are already a part of your reality – even if they are not. Here are a few examples just to get you started:

1. My mind is wonderful.
2. My energy is addicting and fantastic.
3. All good things come my way without exceptions.
4. Whatever I attract, I become.
5. I feel constantly happy and fulfilled with my life.

You have the creative freedom to add anything you want to this list – the longer and more specific you make it, the better. Do this exercise every day so you can start feeling the results very soon!

MY POSITIVE AFFIRMATIONS

_____

_____

_____

_____

_____

_____

_____

_____

_____

_____

_____

_____

_____

_____

_____

EXERCISE 21
GRATITUDE JOURNALING

For the second exercise, you are going to need a journal. This can be a regular notepad, a real journal, or even the notes app on your phone. As long as it is something where you can write constantly and go back to see what you've written, you're good. To get started, you can also use the worksheet below.

Take a pen and start writing. I suggest you do this every day. Notice everything happening around you and to you - and accentuate the positive each time. Even on those uneventful days where nothing really happens, it is your task in this exercise to find something for which you are grateful. At the end of each day, write down all the things you're grateful for that day. Allow this to become a practice. Try not to skip a day. Remember that being grateful doesn't necessarily mean something good has happened. You should always be grateful for the things you already have and who you already are.

For example, you can be grateful for another good day where you learned how to master your negative emotions. You can be grateful for everything you already have in life – a healthy body, mind, family, friends, etc. Or you can even be grateful for the small things in life that actually make a lot of difference – like a sunny day or if someone holds an elevator door for you. This gratitude journaling exercise can help you look at all the positive things in life. By writing them down, you focus on them so much more that, before you know it, this will become your default way of thinking.

Date: _____

Today I am Grateful for... _____

_____

_____

_____

Date: _____

Today I am Grateful for... _____

_____

_____

_____

Date: _____

Today I am Grateful for... _____

_____

_____

_____

Date: _____

Today I am Grateful for... _____

_____

_____

_____

Date: _____

Today I am Grateful for... _____

_____

_____

_____

Date: _____

Today I am Grateful for... _____

_____

_____

_____

Date: _____

Today I am Grateful for... _____

_____

_____

_____

Date: _____

Today I am Grateful for... _____

_____

_____

_____

Date: _____

Today I am Grateful for... _____

_____

_____

_____

Date: _____

Today I am Grateful for... _____

_____

_____

_____

Date: _____

Today I am Grateful for... _____

_____

_____

_____

Date: _____

Today I am Grateful for... _____

_____

_____

_____

Take Care of Your Body

A healthy mind requires a healthy body. These are words to live by. As someone who has invested so much into dealing with your emotions, realizing how to keep them going is the most challenging thing. What not many young people realize is that exercise does you a lot of good – not just for the body, but for the mind as well. There are a few things in life that are always a recommended option, and physical activity is one of them.

To take care of your body means to treat it with caution. Listen to it every time it tries to tell you that it's full when it comes to food, that it needs a stretch when you've been sitting down for too long, and that it is time for a little bit of pampering after a long day of studying. DBT focuses mostly on the mind, but it is always important to keep up with your body too. And to get into that, it is important to follow the next exercise.

EXERCISE 22
BUILDING AN EXERCISE ROUTINE

As soon as you start thinking about getting active, here is an exercise that can help you get in the right mindset. Start by looking into some options. When it comes to working out, think about what you like – is it cardio exercises, weightlifting, running, yoga, pilates, swimming, or something completely different?

Pick something that you want, something that you enjoy, something you feel good about. Then, just start doing it. I know it sounds pretty simple, but when you come to think of it, it really is! Dedicate at least 10-15 minutes at first, just to get into the routine, and then start dedicating some more time from your day to it.

After a while, you will start feeling like you have support – something that helps you be even more focused on the positive. Taking care of your body instantly puts you in a good mood, and after a while, you can see how that reflects on the outside, too. Write down every exercise you do, write down how many times a week you've exercised, and write down how it made you feel to work out to such an extent that you now feel spectacular!

This exercise is designed to help you exercise and give you the most out of your journey to create the most spectacular version of yourself!

_____

_____

_____

_____

What Did You Learn From This Chapter?

It is time to close another chapter filled with extremely powerful DBT skills! I know that this one was a tad longer and a little denser with information, so let's try to take out the best from it. Here is a little summary of what you learned in this chapter:

- ✧ What is emotional regulation, and how does it affect your overall quality of life.
- ✧ Opposite reaction and how to take control of yourself.
- ✧ Solving issues by focusing on the facts – giving yourself clarity in situations when your judgment seems clouded.
- ✧ The power of positivity.
- ✧ The power of exercise on your overall emotional and mental state.

In this chapter, I covered everything about managing your emotions and keeping up with the positive things in life. After you turn this page, a different world awaits! The next part is all about interpersonal effectiveness – from social skills to boundaries. It is time for you to discover the final aspect of DBT so you can shine! Let's go into the details and round up our incredible journey together!

Part 4

INTERPERSONAL EFFECTIVENESS

*"To effectively communicate, we must
realize that we are all different in the way we
perceive the world and use this understanding
as a guide to our communication with others."*

– Tony Robbins

Together, we have come to the last part of this book. So far, DBT has taught you plenty, but now, it is time to take all that knowledge that was always within you and turn to the final bit – interpersonal effectiveness and how to use it. During this part, you will notice what it is like to work on some aspects of your personality you might not have thought about until now. It is time to focus on what you can improve –yourself. Through the power of interpersonal effectiveness, you will become the version of yourself you're striving toward.

But for now, maybe one thing is on your mind only – what is interpersonal effectiveness? I took the liberty of explaining that to you before we go into further detail.

What is Interpersonal Effectiveness?

When it comes to relationships, everyone can be tricky. Even when considering the relationship, you are developing with yourself, you need to work hard – because you can be tricky, too. The trickiness part comes from the fact that not everyone knows how to use the power of the wise mind. Because as soon as it becomes a part of a relationship, you know you are in for constructive communication. Constructive communication is the key to success in all your relationships – with yourself, your family, friends, etc.

With this in mind, interpersonal effectiveness is about asking what you want or even saying no to someone while keeping your self-respect and the relationship intact. It is all about having a conversation (a relationship) with someone; no matter the outcome, you still feel good about yourself. Interpersonal effectiveness does not mean you need to twist your words and be diplomatic every time until you get what you want. It does not even mean you should get what you want every time. But it means that you should be happy with the outcome and yourself every time. It is about being proud of how you communicated things to that point where you feel good about yourself but still see the situation objectively. After all, you should not applaud yourself if you mishandle a communication or a relationship issue, right?

Essentially, interpersonal effectiveness means that you have found a calm yet strong way to express your needs while maintaining your integrity. In this case, the most important thing you can do is ask what you want or need and say no to a situation that doesn't suit you.

This entire section is an integral part of DBT because it can show you exactly how you affect your relationships. By now, you know that all communications and relationships are important. But did you know that the outcome of those communications and relationships is important as well? The outcomes affect your well-being, your self-esteem, and your sense of purpose. Now that you know all this, would you still be able to continue your relationships as you did until this point?

Social Skills

A lot of young people don't know how to ask for something, but rather make demands about it. Some adolescents even ask for things in a way that is confusing or don't ask at all. Interpersonal effectiveness skills are helpful here – they can make you focus on the most effective way to create and maintain a relationship. That is why I love this section; it is dedicated to the power of social skills.

Social skills are something everyone has. Some of you may have more of them, some less – but it is ultimately something embedded in our systems as human beings. We all need to communicate and create relationships with other people. This is something that cannot be done without some strong and healthy social skills. Let's explain this a bit better.

Think of any relationship you have as a tree. The better the relationship is, the bigger the tree grows. The stronger it is, the more incredible it looks. But this tree needs a system to support it while it is growing. The roots grow just as much as the leaves! Think of this every time you create or try to maintain a relationship with someone. For that relationship to grow, you need to focus on the roots. DBT, including the social skills, helps you with that. It can help you realize how to build strong roots, maintain relationships, and be effective at it.

The goal is to develop these social skills to help you become a better person. While I would love to get into the DBT interpersonal effectiveness skills right away, let's just look at it from a different angle – from the benefits point of view. Once you develop the social skills you need, here is what you will experience:

1. Improved communication

Considering interpersonal effectiveness means considering another method of communicating your feelings and thoughts clearly and respectfully. When you learn how to express them effectively, you can reduce any misunderstandings you have with the people around you, and you can build stronger and better relationships with everyone. How to do this? Don't worry; this is the part that I decided to focus on the most, and the three exercises cover the three aspects of this. They are *active listening* (when you fully concentrate on the other person and what they are saying, understanding their perspective and all), *resolving conflicts* (this is when you can be assertive and address an issue in a way that is constructive and helps you focus on finding a solution), and *empathy* (this is the part where you are respectful of both yours and the other party's feelings, thoughts, and emotions).

2. Boundaries

Teaching yourself how to establish boundaries in your personal and professional life will help you go a long way in the future. It will also help you understand other people's boundaries as well. This will help you come to terms with yourself and will prevent you from getting into conflicts in interpersonal relationships.

3. Improved self-respect

The DBT skills you will learn here will enhance your self-respect, as you will notice that you make choices that align with your values and self-worth. This will give you the ability to stand up for yourself in tough situations.

4. Less stress, more emotional intelligence

I mentioned empathy just a few sentences before this, and while I have created an entire exercise about it, you need to understand how deeply this will impact you. When you use interpersonal skills and strengthen them, you can navigate through relationships with ease, which will lead to less emotional strain and less anxiety. In turn, this will show great empathy and higher emotional intelligence. You learn how to understand and recognize your emotions and those of the people around you, so don't be afraid to open up!

Let's move on to the exercises for this part.

EXERCISE 23
ROLE-PLAYING – ACTIVE LISTENING

One of the key components of DBT is practicing active listening. Since the exercises here have the objective of helping you create the best version of yourself, I suggest you do some role-play for all the exercises for today. You will need a few materials for this particular one – a quiet space, another person who can help you with the exercise, a timer or a stopwatch, and a scenario (but this is optional).

Before you go into the exercise, it is important to accentuate how helpful active listening is in any relationship. It is more than just hearing the words; it is remembering and responding to them accordingly. This is an essential skill in every DBT aspect, and it can ensure that all misunderstandings are minimal. Active listening includes asking clarifying questions and letting the other person speak while you give them your full and undivided attention.

For this exercise, choose to be the listener, while the person sitting across from you would be the speaker. Then, they will start talking about an issue with you. This can either be an imaginary issue or a real-life issue. Here is an example scenario:

You were organizing a party, and you didn't invite them. Now, you get to hear how they feel and what they think about it. Listen to them talk, but really hear what they have to say. Answer their questions and share your opinion on the topic, too. Talk about your initial responses (especially yours) and note how everything made you feel. Talk about the challenging parts of active listening and what you learned. Also, think about how you can apply this exercise in real life. *Time your responses to a minute or two just so you can avoid getting stuck in unnecessary info.*

There are more scenarios such as this one - here are a few examples just to get you going:

1. You wanted to talk about your feelings, but you got shut out in the middle of the conversation.

2. They felt like you didn't listen to them when they were talking.

3. You were supposed to go to school together, but you forgot to pick them up.

4. You asked them if they wanted to go shopping with you, and they declined.

5. You asked for help from them for a school assignment, and they didn't help you.

They did a favor for you, but never even got a thank you from you.

EXERCISE 24
ROLE-PLAYING – ASSERTIVENESS

The second exercise has a different objective. Assertiveness is something you need to develop if you want to learn how to express your thoughts and feelings directly, respectfully, and honestly. This exercise is about refraining from being aggressive or passive while doing so.

Again, for this exercise, you will need another person who will actively participate. You will need a space where you can do the exercise and a timer so you can time your responses.

Assertiveness is the middle ground in communication. It means setting clear and respectful boundaries. It also means maintaining a steady tone of voice and manner, maintaining eye contact, and being honest yet respectful.

In this situation, you can be both the speaker and the listener. The scenario can be anything you like – from a fictional one to a real-life one. If you are the listener, then you will have to respond to the reaction of the speaker (they choose a scenario where they express a need or stand up for themselves). After you're done, you can switch the roles.

As an example scenario, let's say you borrowed something from them and didn't return it. In this role-playing exercise, you will need to understand the needs of the speaker. Listen to their, "I" statements, where they express their needs and feelings, and adhere to the clear boundaries they set. If you feel like you cannot do the last one, then it is okay to talk about it until you find a middle ground. Throughout the exercise, try to maintain a calm and steady voice and keep eye contact at all times.

Note that, during this exercise, you and the person sitting across from you may not be able to see eye to eye. This role-playing exercise has a goal to provide a realistic response – which may be one of three things – acting positively, asking for further clarification, or acting negatively. But no matter the response, you should maintain the assertiveness.

To make the most out of this exercise, I recommend you be both the listener and the speaker. Here are a few sample scenarios:

1. Trying to refuse a request from the person sitting opposite you.
2. You talked about them behind their back, and they found out, now they're confronting you with it.
3. They treated you unfairly, and now you are confronting them.
4. You try to set boundaries with them.
5. You ask them for help with a certain assignment or homework.
6. They pressured you into staying out later than you were supposed to.

Once the exercise is done, look within and note how you felt when you expressed yourself. Did you learn something about your communication style? How challenging was it for you to maintain your assertiveness at all times? Finally, think about how you can apply assertiveness to your life because you may have just learned something new and positive about yourself through this exercise.

EXERCISE 25
ROLE-PLAYING – EMPATHY

The last exercise from this part is all about empathy. Some of you may already know what empathy is – it is the ability to feel what the other person is feeling. It is the ability to put yourself in their shoes and understand their origin in a certain situation. Empathy is a very important skill that every teenager should develop. That's why I recommend a role-playing exercise here – so you can get the most out of it.

You know the drill – you need another person, a quiet space for the exercise, a partner, and a timer so you can measure your responses. But in this case, the first thing you will do is start discussing the concept of empathy. Empathy is the ability to understand another person's feelings. Also, it is not about fixing an issue or a concern. It is not even about giving advice! Empathy is a part of a healthy relationship and the base for effective communication. It can help a person feel understood and supported.

The components of a conversation filled with empathy include reflecting emotions back to the speaker, avoiding being judgmental or critical, offering validation about their feelings, and listening to them actively. Empathy is an important part of every relationship you form in life, and it can help you in many social interactions.

Create a scenario where the speaker needs support. For example, let's say that the person opposite you is upset because they had an important exam, and they failed it or didn't perform as they expected. This is an emotional thing for them, and it is your job as the listener to hear what they have to say – whether that is anxiety, frustration, anger, sadness, or something else.

It is your job to listen to them attentively while they are speaking. They describe the situation in detail, and it is your job to reflect back to them what they say and offer support. Try to avoid giving them advice as this is not a very good approach. After the time has passed and you shared some empathy with them, switch the roles. It is important for you to understand what it's like to be on both sides of the situation. This way, you will know how it feels, you will know what the most challenging bit was, and you will learn something about yourself – how you handle these kinds of situations and in which areas you can improve. Finally, you will learn how to apply empathy in your real-life relationships.

To get you started, here are a few example scenarios how you can practice that:

1. You failed a test, and you want to talk about it.
2. They are being bullied and they just want you to hear them out, because it is a difficult time for them.
3. You are anxious about a presentation and want to talk about it.
4. They are struggling with body image issues.
5. You simply want to talk about your day and your challenges.

You felt left out in a certain situation and want to be understood.

Setting and Maintaining Boundaries

Boundaries are the limits we set for ourselves in relationships and interactions with others. They define what is acceptable and unacceptable behavior towards us, helping to protect our emotional well-being and maintain healthy relationships. Setting and maintaining boundaries is crucial for everyone, but it can be especially important for teenagers as they navigate friendships, family dynamics, and the pressures of school life.

In DBT, boundaries are seen as essential for emotional regulation, self-respect, and effective interpersonal relationships. Learning how to set and maintain boundaries can help you feel more in control of your life, reduce stress, and prevent feelings of resentment or frustration.

Boundaries can be divided into several categories, each of which plays a vital role in maintaining healthy relationships:

Physical boundaries: These relate to your personal space and physical comfort. They determine how close others can get to you physically and what kind of physical contact is acceptable. For example, you might feel uncomfortable with hugging someone you don't know well or prefer to have your own space when studying.

Emotional boundaries: These involve your feelings and emotions. Emotional boundaries protect your emotional well-being by helping you avoid being overwhelmed by others' emotions or taking on their problems as your own. For example, you might set a boundary by telling a friend that you're not comfortable discussing a certain topic that triggers anxiety for you.

Intellectual boundaries: These involve your thoughts, ideas, and beliefs. Intellectual boundaries protect your right to have your own opinions and beliefs and to respect those of others. For example, you might set a boundary by asking someone not to criticize your ideas or beliefs in a disrespectful way.

Time boundaries: These involve how you manage your time and prioritize your activities. Time boundaries protect your time by helping you balance different aspects of your life, such as school, extracurricular activities, and social life. For example, you might set a boundary by saying no to a social invitation because you need to study or rest.

Material boundaries: These involve your personal belongings and financial resources. Material boundaries protect your possessions and money by ensuring that they are used or shared in ways that you're comfortable with. For example, you might set a boundary by not lending your favorite book to someone who tends to lose things.

Setting these boundaries is essential for several reasons:

Self-respect: Boundaries help you show respect for yourself by acknowledging your own needs and limits. When you set boundaries, you say your comfort and well-being matter.

Emotional protection: Boundaries protect you from being overwhelmed by others' demands or emotions. They allow you to take care of your own emotional needs first, so you don't burn out or become resentful.

Healthy relationships: Boundaries are the foundation of healthy relationships. They help ensure that both you and others know what is expected and what is off-limits, reducing misunderstandings and conflicts.

Stress reduction: Clear boundaries reduce stress by preventing you from taking on too much responsibility or feeling pressured to meet others' expectations. This can lead to a more balanced and fulfilling life.

Since boundaries are an important part of life, it is imperative to know how to implement them. These can help you grow into the person you want to be. Let's move on to the exercise bit.

EXERCISE 26
BOUNDARY-SETTING

The first exercise is all about creating healthy boundaries. If you do not know how to properly place them in your life, let me remind you that you are not the only one. Many people, such as yourself, are probably struggling to do the same. But the difference is that you have this book in your arsenal – one you can easily pass on to someone you notice is in need of it. In DBT, setting and maintaining healthy boundaries is an essential part of becoming a strong version of yourself. That is why this exercise is crucial.

You will need a pen and paper to write things down, and other than that, you're good to go! Before you start writing things down, understand that boundaries are exceptionally important. They are the limit that can help you protect yourself from any emotional, mental, and physical damage. They can help you manage your relationships with yourself and the people around you – mostly because they are based on mutual respect and understanding.

Write down all the times you felt like someone challenged you to do something that is out of your comfort zone – for example, when you hung out with your friends, and they dared you to do something you didn't really like doing. That is your boundary. You probably didn't want to say no to that just because you didn't want to look like a coward or a weak person at the moment, but deep down, you knew that it was not something you liked doing. Write about how you would react if you knew that you could set a boundary at the moment. Would anything be different?

Reflect on that – how would it feel to set a boundary? Would it feel like something you can gain confidence from? Or would it feel like a big challenge? Remember that the good thing about challenging yourself, in this case, is that you not only learn new things about yourself but also learn how you may handle a situation in which you are expected to do one thing but would prefer to do the complete opposite.

Think about the aspects of your life for which you want to set boundaries. For example, these aspects may be connected to school, to your friends, or even to yourself. Setting a boundary is not an action you do only once – it is a continuous process you will keep doing – it requires ongoing attention. While you write down the things you are setting boundaries to keep a note that you will constantly need to remind yourself how to practice them, and basically focus on taking care of yourself.

_____

_____

_____

_____

_____

_____

_____

_____

_____

_____

_____

_____

_____

_____

_____

_____

_____

_____

_____

_____

_____

_____

_____

_____

_____

_____

_____

_____

_____

_____

_____

_____

_____

_____

_____

_____

_____

_____

_____

_____

_____

_____

_____

_____

_____

_____

_____

_____

_____

_____

_____

EXERCISE 27
BOUNDARY COMMUNICATION

It is one thing to set boundaries for yourself, but it is a completely different thing to try to communicate those boundaries with the people around you. If you want to practice effectively communicating these boundaries, DBT suggests you practice that. Because no matter what you do in life, practice makes it perfect. You need to know how to empower yourself and clearly express your boundaries at every given moment. That is why this exercise is created solely for that intention.

For this exercise, I recommend that you sit down with someone (maybe a parent or an older sibling) so you can fully grasp the scope of what it is you are trying to do. The exercise is a conversation with them where you express your feelings. Try to sit them down and explain what is happening – how you feel, what makes you uncomfortable, or what awakens some negative emotions or thoughts within. Stay focused on the topic and be assertive. Let them know that your final goal is to know how to communicate your boundaries.

Now, think about an aspect of your life where you want to set a boundary. This could be anything – something that has been bothering you, something that has been making you uncomfortable, or something you've wanted to change. Talk to them and explain the entire situation. For example, this can be trying to stop someone at school from bullying you. While you are explaining, use a calm tone and a steady voice. I know this may be difficult for you at first but think about what you may gain from it. These exercises are designed solely for your consideration and are here to help you improve. And in time, after practicing them, you will.

Now, after you've communicated your issue, I recommend grabbing a pen and paper and writing down how the conversation made you feel. Did you feel confident about it? What was the most challenging part of the process? Would you think that, in real life, when you communicate this, you might get a response that would put you back to square one? If so, how would you react to prevent yourself from going back? It is through these questions of self-reflection that you will be able to learn how to better stand up for yourself and know how to deal with future situations.

_____

_____

_____

_____

_____

_____

_____

_____

_____

_____

_____

_____

_____

_____

_____

_____

_____

_____

_____

_____

_____

_____

_____

_____

_____

_____

_____

The DBT interpersonal effectiveness skills are the final part we are going to cover in this book. They are specifically designed to help you get what you need from a relationship while being respectful of yourself and the people around you. Relationships can be very challenging and tricky, and at any point, you might come face to face with some unstable and extremely negative emotions.

That is why I am sharing the effectiveness tools: DEAR MAN, GIVE, and FAST.

Objectives Effectiveness: DEAR MAN

Starting from the first one, DEAR MAN is something that can help you achieve a certain goal or objective – no matter what that is. As you can probably notice, DEAR MAN is an acronym, and it stands for:

Describe the current situation

Express your feelings

Assert yourself

Reinforce

stay **M**indful

Appear confident

Negotiate

When it comes to the use of DEAR MAN, you first need to make sure of what you want. The clarity of your argument will be based on the clarity of your thoughts. So, if you want to start determining what you want or need, give some time to your priorities. It's okay that, at certain times in life, you feel overwhelmed. But this feeling of being overwhelmed can help you remove all the low-priority demands. Start considering doing things only because you want to do them, not because you *should* do them.

Also, consider asking for help when you need it. At the end of the day, you need to come to terms with the fact that you don't have to do everything yourself. You can even use the DEAR MAN to ask someone else for help – it all depends on your goals. Here are some goals that you might have in mind:

1. You want to stand up for your rights and want to be taken seriously.
2. You want to resolve a conflict.
3. You want to have your opinions and thoughts to be taken seriously.
4. You want to request something from someone in a way that they will do it.
5. You want to refuse to be a part of an unreasonable situation and refuse a certain request.

However, there is something to remember here. Even with the DEAR MAN technique, note that you can't have it your way all the time. You can't get everything from people constantly. Sometimes, your techniques will be put to the test, and you will need to increase your interpersonal skills; other times, they will fail completely. That's okay. In these situations, it is important to go back to distress tolerance because you know that what you want is impossible to get.

While this is a little bit tricky to understand right now, I have created an exercise for each of these techniques. That will give you the clarity you need.

EXERCISE 28
DEAR MAN

What's interesting about all these exercises is that no matter what you want to achieve, you always go back to the wise mind I mentioned at the beginning of the book. There is no better mindset than the wise mind, so whenever you want to do this exercise, go into that state and then begin.

For this exercise, you will need a pen and paper and a friend, sibling or parent – someone you completely trust. Take the pen and paper and write out the acronym vertically. Each letter represents a certain aspect you're going to focus on. This way, you will have the opportunity to spend as much time as you need on the most challenging letter. Before you begin, make sure you are comfortable.

Sit down with the person you've chosen to be your partner and think of a situation you want to discuss. Start from the beginning – here is an example of how the conversation should flow:

Let's say you sat down with a friend who gave you a hard time and maybe even made fun of you in front of other people. Now, start going through the letters.

D – Describe the situation from your point of view and clarify what you are asking them. In this case, you're asking them not to do that to you anymore. But, since you are wise, try to only state the facts. That means you have to limit yourself to not judging the situation, who and what caused it, and whether it is good or bad.

E – Express your feelings about the situation. Avoid transferring the blame to them but let them know how you feel. Go from the assumption that they don't know how you feel (because that is usually the case). Think of this as your opportunity to openly tell them how you feel.

A – Assert yourself – tell them what you want. In this case, you want to stop being made fun of in front of other people. Be clear and concise so that there is no misunderstanding. Do not assume that the person sitting across from you is able to read your mind.

R – Reinforce your statement. That way, you will make sure there is a positive outcome to your request. I recommend that you reinforce there would be a positive outcome if they agree with you and a negative outcome if they don't – that way, you are more likely to get an affirmative response.

M – Mindfulness of your goal. The person sitting across from you will not be mindful of your goal – that's why you should do that yourself. Don't get distracted from the conversation and, if you need to, start repeating things – be just like a broken record. If they attack you, ignore their attacks. Repeat yourself until you make your point and notice they have understood you.

A – Appear confident, as if you are in charge of the situation. You may not be at first, but you will lean into it as time passes. Exude confidence in your posture, your tone of voice, and your words.

N – Negotiating is key. You can be as confident as you want, but you also need to be flexible. If you want to get something, you need to be willing to give something, too. Focus on your goal but be practical about what will work. Make way for communication and find a mutual solution to the issue.

Just to help you get going, here are 5 example scenarios:

Asking to spend some more time together.

Ask them for some extra help on something.

Ask to spend less time together.

You feel like you need to raise a particular subject with them and talk about it.

Ask them to include you more in their social activities

Describe the Situation _____

_____

_____

Express Your Feelings _____

_____

_____

Assert Yourself _____

_____

_____

Reinforce Your Statement _____

_____

_____

Mindfulness _____

_____

_____

Appear Confident _____

_____

_____

Negotiate _____

_____

_____

D _____

_____

_____

E _____

_____

_____

A _____

_____

_____

R _____

_____

_____

M _____

_____

_____

A _____

_____

_____

N _____

_____

_____

D _____

_____

_____

E _____

_____

_____

A _____

_____

_____

R _____

_____

_____

M _____

_____

_____

A _____

_____

_____

N _____

_____

_____

D _____

_____

_____

E _____

_____

_____

A _____

_____

_____

R _____

_____

_____

M _____

_____

_____

A _____

_____

_____

N _____

_____

_____

D _____

_____

_____

E _____

_____

_____

A _____

_____

_____

R _____

_____

_____

M _____

_____

_____

A _____

_____

_____

N _____

_____

_____

D _____

_____

_____

E _____

_____

_____

A _____

_____

_____

R _____

_____

_____

M _____

_____

_____

A _____

_____

_____

N _____

_____

_____

Relationship Effectiveness: GIVE

Let's move on to the second exercise, which is all about relationship effectiveness. I cannot remind you enough how challenging it can be to deal with unstable emotions. During these times, one wrong step in communication can damage a relationship beyond repair. That is why the technique GIVE will provide you with the help you need to keep your relationship intact, even in those times when you have an argument.

GIVE is another acronym that will help you obtain some skills that are important for all those times when you don't know how to act in an argument but still want to meet your goal or objective. Each letter represents a certain aspect you're going to focus on. Here is what GIVE stands for:

Gentle

Interested

Validate

Easy manner

To provide you with a little more clarity on this one, think of the GIVE as a how skill and of DEAR MAN as a what skill. DEAR MAN is more about what you do, and GIVE is more about how you do it (the same thing will apply to FAST, but more on that later on. However, since all these skills are connected, you will subconsciously improve your DEAR MAN skills by using the GIVE skills.

A part of the relationship effectiveness is to tend to your relationships as regularly as you can. You should not allow any issues or troubles to pop up and should remain there – like an elephant in the room. Instead, GIVE is your opportunity to address them as soon as they happen. By doing this, you use all the skills you've learned from this book to prevent any issues from becoming bigger and eventually blowing up. This technique also helps you end any toxic relationships because it shows you it is not necessarily a good thing to continue doing something you don't want and give a person the attention they probably don't deserve.

GIVE is, just like DEAR MAN, all about goals. Before you start your communication, it is important to be clear about what you want. Sometimes, you may want a person to accept you more. You may want to stop them from rejecting or criticizing you as much. Some of the goals you may have in mind include the following:

1. You want to act in a certain way so the other person will give you what you want.

2. You want to act in a certain way so the other person will not feel wrong about you rejecting their requests.

3. You want to act in a certain way to balance the good of the short-term goals with the good of the long-term goals.

So, you see – this one is all about balancing your relationships with the goals you have for yourself and your life. You should not sacrifice who you are just to get the respect of others – which, at the end of the day, you probably don't even need. The only time you should commit to something is when you want to. As we lean into GIVE and learn the FAST technique, you will see how these three techniques should be used at the same time and balanced effectively.

EXERCISE 29
GIVE

For this exercise, think about how you want to be treated in a situation during a discussion. Do you want to be yelled at, or do you want to be treated with kindness? How would you imagine the conversation will flow if you want to be treated with kindness? This exercise consists of you getting a pen and paper, as well as someone to discuss with. Here is how you can use the acronym.

First, write it down on your piece of paper.

G – Remind yourself that people respond in a gentle manner better than they do to yelling. That's why, no matter what you want to discuss, as long as you present it well and approach them with kindness and respect, you know you have opened a steady line for communication. Avoid being snarky, making threats, and passing judgment on them. Tolerate it if they want to say no to you and give them time to respond to what you said to them.

I – Being interested is another thing you should focus on. Has it ever happened to you that sometimes someone doesn't listen to a word you say? You see their attention is being pulled to a different side, and you get a little angry about it. Well, you should give as much as you get. Being interested may be a challenging thing for you, but in this case, it is only fair to listen to their point of view, too. Maintain eye contact, don't interrupt them, and carefully listen to what they have to say.

V – Show the other person that you've listened to their side of the story by completely understanding them. Validate their point of view and try to put yourself in their shoes. Even in those times when you think they aren't making much sense, try to find the grain of truth and reason for what they are saying. Be non-judgmental and be that in a loud way. Validate their feelings, wants, opinions, and difficulties (which, remember, does not mean you have to accept them). Oftentimes, someone just needs to feel heard and seen, and that paves the way for a potentially solid relationship.

E – Easy manner means trying to be as friendly and as easy-going as you possibly can be. You can even use humor to ease into the conversation and relax the other person. You should not guilt-trip them but rather have a good attitude, especially if the other person may feel hurt by your request. Give your best to accept their response and maintain calmness.

Here are a few scenarios to get you started:

1. Support your friend when they're having a bad time.
2. Resolving a conflict you may have with them.
3. Comforting them after they get a bad grade.
4. Talking about a sensitive issue.
5. Helping them whenever they feel anxious about something.

Gentle _____

_____

_____

Interested _____

_____

_____

Validate _____

_____

_____

Easy Manner _____

_____

_____

G _____

_____

I _____

_____

V _____

_____

E _____

_____

G _____

_____

I _____

_____

V _____

_____

E _____

_____

G _____

_____

I _____

_____

V _____

_____

E _____

_____

G _____

_____

I _____

_____

V _____

_____

E _____

_____

G _____

_____

I _____

_____

V _____

_____

E _____

_____

G _____

_____

I _____

_____

V _____

_____

E _____

_____

Self-Respect Effectiveness: FAST

The last technique is FAST. It is very easy to get lost in the moment and lose yourself in the whirlpool of emotions while you are having a conversation or an argument with someone. And before you know it, you have bent to their will without ever having the intention of doing that. This is where the last technique – FAST, comes into the picture. As you can see, it is a self-respecting effectiveness skill, and it is one we will dissect together in depth. FAST can help you maintain your self-respect during a discussion, conversation, or argument with someone.

Yes, you guessed it, this is an acronym as well. It will teach you how to act every time you are faced with a challenging situation, yet you are determined to meet your goals without sacrificing yourself in the process. Here is what FAST stands for:

be **F**air

no **A**pologies

Stick to values

be **T**ruthful

I mentioned earlier that FAST is just like GIVE – it is a part of the how skills that will help you have an objective and successful discussion. For this technique, you must remember that nobody can take away your self-respect – unless you give it up willingly. I noticed something, especially with young people such as yourself, that self-respect is based on the quality of your relationships with other people. By using this skill, you learn how to tend to your relationships skillfully.

As with the two previous techniques, before you begin your conversation, you need to keep your goal in mind. Doing this will help you remain focused and clear on what you want. And remember, the focus here is maintaining your level of self-respect. With that in mind, here are a few goals as an example for you:

1. You want to like yourself.
2. You want to feel effective and capable.
3. You want to act in a way that makes you feel moral, respected, and valued.

Before we move on to the exercise, I would like to share the wise words of Eleanor Roosevelt – *"No one can make you feel inferior without your consent."*

EXERCISE 30
FAST

We have made our way to the last exercise of the book – and boy, is it a good one! For this final exercise, you will need to practice in the same way you practiced with the other two exercises – you need a pen and paper and someone to talk to. Again, you can choose anyone you want – it can be a sibling, a parent, or a friend. Only this time, note that it's helpful to practice FAST when you're not in the middle of an argument so you can first get used to it. Then, as you do, you can start using it in real-life situations when things get a little more intense.

Take out your pen and paper, write the acronym vertically, and go through the letters one by one.

F – it is all about being fair. When you think of a situation you want to discuss with the person sitting opposite you, you need to be fair when describing it. After all, while you still want to put whatever it is you feel or think about the situation on the table, you still need to be mindful of their wants and needs, too. Stick to the facts and avoid judgment but remain fair to yourself.

A – if you don't have to, don't apologize. Putting yourself in a position when you want to ask for something is not a reason to apologize. Having a different opinion or a point of view is also not a reason to apologize. It is okay for you to take up space. The only situation where you need to apologize is when you have made a mistake and want to get things right. Apologizing means you are wrong. Taking up space and having an opinion is not wrong. Apologizing for doing all this will only make you lower your self-worth and self-respect. Also, it gets on other people's nerves.

S – stick to your values as much as you can. I know that it can be scary to ask for a change (or to ask for anything, for that matter). At the time, it might feel like the person you're talking to may stop liking you if you ask them for something. Through my years of experience, I have noticed that this is often the case, especially with young people – and that is why I am accentuating it now. Don't let fear be the overwhelming feeling, and don't compromise just to avoid conflict or to please the other person. Doing this will only make you like yourself less in the long run.

T – lastly, make sure you are always truthful to yourself. Stick to the facts and avoid stretching them out too thin. If you start noticing a dishonesty pattern within yourself, remember to cut it out. In the long run, this pattern will make you like yourself less and less and will diminish your self-respect. There is no need to make judgmental statements – only the facts are enough. Also, being truthful means being grounded and not acting helpless. Even in those times when you feel insecure and scared, try to stand firmly on the ground with both feet.

Here are a few example scenarios to get you started:

1. Trying to say no to peer pressure.
2. Make your voice heard in a group project, where you only know the person sitting opposite you.
3. Asking more time to finish a task.
4. Dealing with unwanted criticism.
5. Setting boundaries with the person sitting opposite you.

With FAST, there are some instances where being truthful may be a destructive thing for the relationship. To guide yourself through this tricky process, I suggest you include a wise mind to guide you whenever you feel like it is appropriate to do so.

It is incredibly interesting to learn that these techniques are part of what makes you an incredible, stable, calm, and happy person. I would love to see you give them all a go because there is so much you can learn about yourself from them!

Be **F**air _____

_____

No **A**pologies _____

_____

Stick to Values _____

_____

Be **T**ruthful _____

_____

F _____

_____

A _____

_____

S _____

_____

T _____

_____

F _____

_____

A _____

_____

S _____

_____

T _____

_____

F _____

_____

A _____

_____

S _____

_____

T _____

_____

F _____

_____

A _____

_____

S _____

_____

T _____

_____

F _____

_____

A _____

_____

S _____

_____

T _____

_____

What Did You Learn From This Chapter?

As the final chapter in the book, I believe that things are wrapping up quite nicely. I know this was a long one and that we had a lot to cover here, so let's do a short recap of everything you learned through this chapter, shall we?

- ✧ What is interpersonal effectiveness.
- ✧ Social skills and the power of creating and maintaining relationships.
- ✧ What you will gain by developing your social skills.
- ✧ The power of boundaries; different types of boundaries – why setting them and maintaining them is important.
- ✧ The first of the three techniques – DEAR MAN – is all about the effectiveness of objectives.
- ✧ The second of the three techniques – GIVE – is all about the effectiveness of relationships.
- ✧ The third of the three techniques – FAST – is all about the effectiveness of self-respect.

This chapter may have been the longest one, but it was essential to go through it together so I could help you go through this wonderful journey to yourself. All of the techniques you've learned here are something that will soon become invaluable to you. I know it will be difficult to deal with them at first – it may have seemed like the more you read this book, the more challenges you will have. But there is nothing better than stepping out of your comfort zone when you know it is the path toward creating the best version of yourself.

That being the case, I can't wait for you to turn the page so we can complete our time together on a high note!

CONCLUSION

Congratulations! You've made it to the end of this book! I am happy to say, however, that your journey to your true self is something that will continue long after you've completed reading this. I wouldn't even be surprised if you come back to the book every once in a while. By exploring and practicing the skills of DBT, you will take a significant step toward understanding yourself better, managing your emotions more effectively, and building healthier relationships (with yourself and the people around you). This is no small feat—learning and applying DBT skills takes courage, dedication, and a willingness to grow. You should be incredibly proud of yourself.

Take a moment to reflect on everything you learned in this book. Think back to when you first started reading this book. Do you feel like you can face some life challenges better now? Do you think you have a better scope of your emotions? How have you changed through this book? How can you manage your life better from now on?

Up until this point, you may have been faced with times when you didn't know how to react or hoped for a different outcome than the one you got. That's okay. Learning how to get through these situations equals growth. What matters here is that you are committed to learning and applying these skills, every time things are hard.

The skills you've learned in this book are tools that you can carry with you for the rest of your life. They're not just for times of crisis or extreme emotion; they can be integrated into your everyday routines, helping you to live more mindfully, manage stress, and communicate more effectively. But, to make the most out of them, you need to know how to make that happen.

Try to practice these skills as often as you can. For them to become a part of who you are, you need to practice them as often as possible. Set some time aside every day and revise the techniques you've learned here. The more you practice them, the easier they will be for you.

Practice with mindfulness. As you learned in the book, mindfulness is the foundation of DBT, and to take full advantage of this, you need to keep being fully present and remove judgment from your thoughts and feelings. Use the toolbox of skills you've taken from this book every time you face a challenge. Consider how you can make the most out of each situation.

Reflect on your past experiences and notice how you start to use the DBT skills in your life. Put some finishing touches and keep moving forward while constantly evaluating your progress. Also, don't forget to ask for help when needed. If you feel like you need some assistance in overcoming a challenging situation, remember that you are not alone. You can always come back to this book and revisit a chapter or a segment alone, or with a friend, sibling or anyone you like.

As you continue to grow and develop, remember that the skills you've learned in this book are just the beginning. Life is full of opportunities for learning and self-improvement. By staying open to new experiences and challenges, you'll continue to build resilience, deepen your self-awareness, and strengthen your relationships.

DBT is not about perfection; it's about progress. It's about finding a balance between accepting yourself as you are and striving to become the person you want to be. It's about understanding that you have the power to shape your own life, even in the face of adversity.

You've embarked on a journey that many never take — self-improvement and emotional growth. You've shown that you're willing to face your challenges head-on, learn new coping methods, and build a life that reflects your values and aspirations. This is a remarkable achievement, and it's something you can carry with you as you move forward in life.

As you close this book, know that the skills you've learned are yours to keep. They are tools that can help you navigate the many twists and turns that life will inevitably bring. Whenever you face a new challenge or feel uncertain about the future, remember the progress and strength you've discovered within yourself.

You are capable, resilient, and worthy of the life you want to create. Keep believing in yourself, practicing your skills, and moving forward. The journey doesn't end here — it's just the beginning. Your future is full of possibilities, and you have the tools to make the most of them.

Thank you for allowing this book to be a part of your journey. Wishing you all the best as you continue to grow, learn, and thrive.

THANK YOU

Thank you so much for purchasing my book.

The marketplace is filled with dozens and dozens of other similar books, but you took a chance and chose this one. I hope it was well worth it.

So again, THANK YOU for getting this book and for making it all the way to the end.

Before you go, I wanted to ask you for one small favor.

Could you please consider posting a review for my book on the platform? Posting a review is the best and easiest way to support the work of independent authors like me.

Your feedback will help me to keep writing the kind of books that will help you get the results you want. It would mean a lot to me to hear from you.

Leave a Review on Amazon US →

Leave a Review on Amazon UK →

ABOUT THE AUTHOR

Emily Carter is an author who loves helping teens with their biggest turning point in life, adulting. She grew up in *New York* and is happily married to her high school sweetheart. She also has two of her own children.

In her free time, *Emily* is an avid volunteer at a local food bank and enjoys hiking, traveling, and reading books on personal development. With over a decade of experience in the education and parenting field she has seen the difference that good parenting and the right tips can make in a teenager's life. She is now an aspiring writer through which she shares her insights and advice on raising happy, healthy, and resilient children, teens, and young adults.

Emily's own struggles with navigating adulthood and overcoming obstacles inspired her to write. She noticed a gap in education regarding teaching essential life skills to teens and young adults. She decided to write comprehensive guides covering everything from money and time management to job searching and communication skills. Emily hopes her book will empower teens and young adults to live their best lives and reach their full potential.

To find more of her books, visit her Amazon Author page at:

https://www.amazon.com/author/emily-carter

REFERENCES

Barila, A. (2020) *How To: Effectively Set Boundaries*. Therapy With AB. Available: https://www. therapywithab.com/blog/2020/10/12/how-to-effectively-set-boundaries

Bariso, J. (2019) *28 Emotional Intelligence Quotes That Can Help Make Emotions Work For You, Instead Of Against You*. Inc. Available: https://www.inc.com/justin-bariso/28-emotional-intelligence-quotes-that-can-help-make-emotions-work-for-you-instead-of-against-you.html

Butler, A. (2024) *How To Access Your Intuitive Knowing, Or "Wise Mind"*. Available: https://www. sagetherapy.com/post/how-to-access-your-intuitive-knowing-or-wise-mind

Center Stone. (2024) *Healthy Vs. Unhealthy Coping Mechanisms*. Available: https://centerstone. org/our-resources/health-wellness/substance-use-disorder-healthy-vs-unhealthy-coping-mechanisms/

Charlie Health. (2023) *Check The Facts DBT*. Available: https://www.charliehealth.com/post/check-the-facts-dbt

Counceling Center. (2024) *DBT Skill Radical Acceptance: For Mental Health Healing*. Available: https://counselingcentergroup.com/dbt-skill-radical-acceptance/

Cuncic, A. (2024) *How To Embrace Radical Acceptance*. Very Well Mind. Available: https://www. verywellmind.com/what-is-radical-acceptance-5120614#toc-how-to-practice-radical-acceptance

Da Costa, J. (2023) *Self-Soothe DBT Skills: Sensory Strategies For Distress Tolerance*. Center For DBT. Available: https://centerforcbt.org/2023/11/06/self-soothe-dbt-skills/

DBT Tools. (2024) *Emotional Regulation Skills*. Available: https://dbt.tools/emotional_regulation/index. php

DBTSelfHelp.com. (2024) *How Skills: One-Mindfully, Non-Judgmentally, Effectively*. Available: https:// dbtselfhelp.com/how-skills-one-mindfully-non-judgmentally-effectively/

DBTSelfHelp.com. (2024) *Objectives Effectiveness: Dear Man*. Available: https://dbtselfhelp.com/ objectives-effectiveness-dear-man/

DBTSelfHelp.com. (2024) Pros And Cons. Available: https://dbtselfhelp.com/pros-and-cons/

DBTSelfHelp.com. (2024) *Relationship Effectiveness: Give*. Available: https://dbtselfhelp.com/ relationship-effectiveness-give/#google_vignette

DBTSelfHelp.com. (2024) *Self-Respect Effectiveness: Fast*. Available: https://dbtselfhelp.com/self-respect-effectiveness-fast/

DBTSelfHelp.com. (2024) *What Skills: Observe, Describe, Participate*. Available: https://dbtselfhelp.com/what-skills-observe-describe-participate/

Dialectical Behavior Therapy. (2024) *DBT Distress Tolerance: Exercises, Videos, And Worksheets*. Available: https://dialecticalbehaviortherapy.com/distress-tolerance/

Grouport Therapy. (2024) *Inspiring Quotes To Live By: Embracing DBT Skills For Personal Growth And Transformation*. Available: https://www.grouporttherapy.com/blog/dialectical-behavior-therapy-quotes

Iraheta, N. (2023) *Four DBT Problem-Solving Techniques*. Health And Healing Therapy. Available: https://www.healthandhealingtherapy.com/dbt-problem-solving-techniques/

Klynn, B. (2021) *Emotional Regulation: Skills, Exercises, And Strategies*. Better Up. Available: https://www.betterup.com/blog/emotional-regulation-skills

Lagace, M. (2024) *91 Mind Quotes To Make You Wiser*. Wisdom Quotes. Available: https://wisdomquotes.com/mind-quotes/

Mindful. (2020) *What Is Mindfulness?* Available: https://www.mindful.org/what-is-mindfulness/

Modern Recovery Services. (2023) *Boundary Setting: Definition, Benefits, And Techniques*. Available: https://modernrecoveryservices.com/wellness/coping/skills/social/boundary-setting/

My Cleveland Clinic. (2022) *Dialectical Behavior Therapy (DBT)*. Available: https://my.clevelandclinic.org/health/treatments/22838-dialectical-behavior-therapy-dbt

Psychiatric Associates. (2024) *How Interpersonal Effectiveness Improves Your Relationships*. Available: https://psychassociates.net/how-interpersonal-effectiveness-improves-your-relationships/

Resource Group. (2024) *The Wise Mind Technique In DBT*. Available: https://resourcegrp.org/blog/what-is-the-wise-mind-technique-in-dbt/

Sunrise. (2017) *DBT Interpersonal Effectiveness Skills: The Guide To Healthy Relationships*. Available: https://sunrisertc.com/interpersonal-effectiveness/

Sunrise. (2017). *DBT Distress Tolerance Skills: Your 6-Skill Guide To Navigate Emotional Crises*. Available: https://sunrisertc.com/distress-tolerance-skills/

Zencare. (2024) *Distract, Relax, And Cope: Distress Tolerance Skills*. Available: https://blog.zencare.co/distract-relax-and-cope-distress-tolerance-skills/

Made in United States
Troutdale, OR
11/17/2024

2492651 2R00097